D0892118

Aimee Semple McPherson

Edna St. Vincent Millay

Dorothy Parker

Amelia Earhart

Martha Graham

Anita Loos

WOMEN

by

George H. Douglas

Saybrook

Publishers

Quotations from copyrighted poetry and prose are acknowledged in this book's "Notes" section, which appears at the end of the volume and constitutes an extension of this copyright page.

Designed by Fred Huffman

Library of Congress Cataloging-in-Publication Data

Douglas, George H., 1934–
Women of the 20s.

Bibliography: p.
1. Women—United States—Bibliography. 2.Women—United States—Social Conditions. 3. United States—Popular culture. I. Title.
HQ1412.D64 1986 016.3054′0973 86–1848
ISBN 0–933071–06–X

ISBN 0–933071–06–X

Saybrook Publishers
4223 Cole Avenue, Suite Four, Dallas, TX 75205

Printed in the United States of America

Distributed by W.W. Norton & Company
500 Fifth Avenue, New York, NY 10110

To
Rosalind

PART ONE
An Introduction to the Women of the Twenties

PART TWO
A Magazine of Inventions

PART THREE
Graphs of the Heart

PART ONE

An Introduction to the Women of the Twenties

How shall I know, unless I go
  To Cairo and Cathay
Whether or not this blessed spot
  Is blest in every way?

Now it may be, the flower for me
  Is this beneath my nose;
How shall I tell, unless I smell
  The Carthaginian rose?

The fabric of my faithful love
  No power shall dim or ravel
Whilst I stay here,—but oh, my dear,
  If I should ever travel!

1

When Lights Began to Show

Because we look *back* on the twenties, we see the decade as a fragile structure of bright and brittle dreams, doomed to collapse. There is a childlike and poignant quality about all that building and buying and busyness, innocently surging along in the shadow of forces which were shaping an ugly, inevitable end. It is difficult now for us to imagine the twenties as anything but a parenthesis, bounded on one side by World War I and on the other by the Depression, enclosing a frenetic attempt to forget the grimness of the past and ignore the catastrophe to come.

So we have come to think of the twenties as a time of boisterous and uninhibited living, a time of foolish satisfaction with the unprecedented social and economic growth which was taking place. But that is an oversimplified picture. The twenties were also a time of powerful expression and spiritual change. The war had brought scepticism, cynicism, morbid introspection in its wake; changing social structures were shifting huge new burdens of responsibility onto the individual; there were crosscurrents of confusion and strong winds of discontent in every department of national life.

Of course the people living in the twenties didn't see themselves as part of a "period" at all—and certainly not as a parenthesis. They saw themselves, just as we do, emerging from a known past and living their way into an uncertain future. As is generally the case, most people were not analyzing their life and times very much, but were more or less unreflectively responding to the demands of society and the impulses of their own hearts. Only a few—the artists and entrepreneurs—were really aware of the broad trends which were shaping their times.

The women sketched in this book were among those who saw their own age with uncommon clarity. But none of them was "merely" an observer; they were enthusiastic participants, every one. Individually and collectively, they reveal the conflicting moods and currents of the twenties, personifying the spirit of that now famous but still mystifying decade. Although their lives span many decades, from before the turn of the century to the present day, each of them, in her career and her character, coincided in some important way with the events and values of the twenties. Their achievements and exploits are not just historical in their interest, by any means, but their lives and works do tell us something fascinating about a much-misunderstood time.

These women were certainly not representative of American women in the twenties. For every Edna Millay

or Amelia Earhart, there were thousands for whom the twenties was a period of frustration and disillusionment—women who passed their lives in textile mills or dime stores or hash houses; women who washed endless diapers on aluminum washboards in pre-electric rural America; women trapped in tedious "comfort" who longed for wider horizons, but could not find the means to change their lives. Even the women who were lucky and happy in the twenties—and there were a lot of these too—are probably not very well represented in this book, for most of the women discussed here had tumultuous, in some cases downright miserable, lives, paying a high price for talent and success.

But if these six are not representative, they are nevertheless symbolic. They reveal dramatically the temper of the twenties, and the experience of women in that time. In part the revelation comes because these women do *not* fit into our preconceived notions of the "roaring" twenties and its reckless flappers.

Who were the "women of the twenties"? All the organs of conservative opinion proclaimed loudly in the twenties that women had changed, become something completely different from what they had always been. Women, they said, were at the vortex of a fiery revolution, part of the new "flaming youth." They bobbed their hair, shortened their skirts, danced into the small hours of the morning; they aggressively pursued sex in the back seats of Model-T Fords, carried flasks of bootleg gin in their garters, and generally thumbed their noses at the staid, conventional worlds of their mothers, turning their backs on the old American virtues of motherhood—apple pie and all.

These are the easy generalizations which have come

down to us, but like all such sweeping characterizations, they are only half-truths. Such overly dramatic snapshots tend to cover up much deeper and more fundamental truths about the women of the period, and about American society as a whole. One essential correction to this oversimplified view of the ungoverned and ungovernable female of the roaring twenties is that the phenomenon was not all that new. American women did not start to make themselves over because of the rumble seat or the revelations of Dr. Freud; nor did their self-discovery follow as a consequence of the nineteenth amendment to the Constitution, which gave them the right to vote in the elections of 1920. No, American women had been changing for at least a decade, and perhaps longer; they had been seeing themselves in a new light, and had been seeking, if not yet demanding, a new image, a new ideal—a new place for women in the scheme of things.

Fashion was an excellent indicator of this transformation. Clothes began to change drastically around 1910, and hair was being bobbed everywhere by 1915. The public was following such trend setters as Irene Castle, who introduced simpler clothes that permitted all sorts of athletic activities—a change conceived not so much in a spirit of revolt as of fun and good times. Slowly, but inexorably, between 1900 and the mid-twenties, the feminine ideal in America underwent a remarkable and virtually complete metamorphosis. At the turn of the century, and in the years just before, the notion of American womanhood had been fixed by Charles Dana Gibson, whose "Gibson girl" (the model for which, fittingly, was his own beautiful young wife) defined the age. All of the women's magazines of the

early twentieth century displayed near-replicas of Gibson's archetypical female: long hair, high brow, precise, anatomically narrow waist, thirty-six inch bust, broad hips, well concealed legs, a maternal and wifely manner. They always appeared aloof and self-contained, seemingly incapable of any immodest or irregular thought or deed.

By the nineteen twenties the Gibson girl had vanished—she began to fade quickly from view as skirts rose after 1915—and in her place was the "flapper," best rendered by John Held, Jr. Held's illustrations, overflowing in the so-called "smart magazines" of the day—magazines like the old *Life* and *Judge* and *College Humor*—gave us a new and presumably uninhibited female, aesthetically less pleasing many would say. The flapper, quite unlike the Gibson girl, cut off her hair, concealed her forehead, flattened her chest, de-emphasized her waist, dieted away her hips, and kept as much of her leg in plain view as possible.

Significantly, it was not the dictates of fashion moguls in New York or Paris which brought about most of the fashion changes of the roaring twenties. It was rather the will of millions of American women. Women simply decided that they wanted looser, freer clothes for more active life-styles, they insisted upon it, and they got it, nearly always in opposition to the invested arbiters of fashion (who, after all, had an interest in using up cloth).

During the first half of the 1920s, skirt length became the boiling point of social revolution. Since 1915 the skirt had drifted slowly upward, almost as if it were following some course of nature, until shortly after World War I, skirt hems were about six or seven inches above the ground. By 1920 it seemed that all restraints had been thrown to the winds: skirts were up another five or six inches. The following year, however, there was a big drop, a last futile effort by the fashion industry. Parisian designers and New York manufacturers conspired to keep the hems down, and briefly they succeeded, but in the fall of 1923 and the spring of 1924 the manufacturers found themselves deluged with complaints from women who just didn't want the things that were on display; they wanted short skirts and they wanted them right away. Every year thereafter, until 1927, when skirts finally reached the knee, determined young women had their way, and overruled the fashion designers by sheer force of numbers.

The shorter skirt was not, of course, the only major development in women's fashions during this period. Everything was being lightened, simplified. Gone forever were the excess layers of petticoats; gone, too, were bloomers, chemises, elaborate, harness-like corsets and stays; in came briefs or panties, then called "step-ins" (which at least one wag contended might just as well be called "step-outs"); gone were cotton stockings and in were lighter and thinner ones of silk or rayon. In 1928 the *Journal of Commerce* declared woefully that the amount of cloth required to make up a woman's complete costume (exclusive of her stockings) had dropped from nineteen and a half yards in 1913 to a mere seven yards in 1928—a remarkable development in only fifteen years.

For a time, heavily painted young women, the extreme flapper types, and even those who merely chose to bob their hair or don short skirts found themselves banned from hotels or fashionable restaurants. But eventually these bans failed and the new fashions stuck. In the summer of

1923, a massive corps of policewomen was sent out to the Lake Michigan beaches of Chicago to arrest young ladies wearing bathing suits without stockings. The following summer, however, all the women on the police force would not have been up to the task. Every woman bathing on the beach was showing her legs, all without a whiff of scandal.

But what did it mean? That women had lost control, that they had cast all morality, all virtue, all feminine restraint to the four winds? Well, many said so, and some continue to say so. On the other hand, an equally convincing body of evidence indicates that the flapper era, except for demonstrating a youthful boisterousness, a newly discovered love of high jinks, was little more than a dramatization of traits that were already present. For the truth is, the "new American woman" had been under development for a long time. Even the Gibson girl, passé as she might have become by 1920, had once been regarded as a model of femininity unknown to older, careworn nations of Europe—she was already "the American girl," a creature that in subtle and sometimes hard-to-explain ways had created a novel social milieu and a completely revolutionary style.

There was something decidedly different about American women, and there had been throughout much of the nineteenth century, if not, indeed, throughout colonial times as well. By the 1830s at least, foreign visitors to our shore began to notice new qualities in the American woman that left them sometimes annoyed and often mystified. Very perceptive European writers like Frances Trollope, in her *Domestic Manners of the Americans,* and Alexis de Tocqueville in his *Democracy in America,* were beginning to notice that American women had developed a tremendous resiliency and social flexibility. Tocqueville, after his year-long tour of the United States in the early 1830s, discovered, much to his amazement, American pioneer women who "after having been brought up amid all the comforts of the large towns of New England, had passed, almost without an intermediate stage, from the wealthy abode of their parents to a comfortless hovel in a forest. Fever, solitude, and a tedious life had not broken their springs of courage." Although they were, said Tocqueville, much more locked into the traditional pattern of matrimony than their European sisters, and thus were somewhat conservative deep down, they were at the same time much more flexible and adaptable.

As the twentieth century began, however, critics of the American scene began trying to explain a wholly new twist in the direction of the American woman, a change that could only have been guessed at in the time of Tocqueville. Beginning around 1910, for example, a new generation of American social critics began to take note of the clear dominance of women over the nation's cultural life, a phenomenon brought about by a sharp schism between practical or commercial realms on the one hand, and "higher," "impractical" realms on the other. In many articles, as well as in books like *America's Coming of Age* (1915), Van Wyck Brooks pointed out that by some complex alchemy, women in America had become complete custodians of the higher culture, so totally preoccupied were males with the worlds of getting and spending, with building railroads, dynamos, and commercial establishments. In Brooks's eyes, the masculine spirit in America had been so exhausted or drained by practical considerations that men had, in effect, given over

to women the guardianship of civilization—of art, of reform, of all advanced thinking.

There were, Brooks naturally admitted, male writers, artists, philosophers—quite a rich crop of them—but they were often specialized, a highbrow tributary of the mainstream. The actual quality of American civilization had become a product of the nation's women, who, even in the Victorian age, could hardly be dismissed as nothing more than housewives and mothers. Everything we know about nineteenth-century American history suggests that the late Victorian mold never did really fit women in America. During the 1880s and 1890s, and even earlier, American women were decidedly restless, active, driven by creative urges, anxious to be seen, heard, involved. Contrary to many pat historical accounts, late Victorian women in this country did not sit by the hearth and wait for things to happen. They traveled, wrote books, put themselves in the vanguard of reform; they went up in balloons, explored Europe on their own, and as soon as it was possible wrested the family car away from the "chauffeur" and drove it recklessly down some country lane or across some unplowed field.

Of course these were the women of middle-class America. The problems of poor women—in urban factories and tenements, in stagnant rural backwaters—and of minority and immigrant women were horrendous. Indeed, much of the energy which women brought to the reform movement was fueled by the sufferings of their disadvantaged sisters, many of whom led lives of hopeless degradation. But although the exposés of the Progressive era made their plight a public scandal, these women were a small segment of the population.

Even today, when so many economic injustices have been eradicated, it is still true that women suffer disproportionately from poverty; women's "liberation" has not helped the poor nearly so much as the not-poor. It is important, then, in looking back on the status of women at the opening of our century, to distinguish between the displaced and ill-used women whose fate was so poignantly symbolized by the 1911 Triangle Shirtwaist fire (in which 145 young women were burned to death in an overcrowded and unsafe garment factory), and those millions more who were making their way boldly into a new and challenging age.

William O'Neill, in his book *The Woman Movement: Feminism in the United States and England*, calls the period between 1890 and 1920 a "kind of feminist golden age. In no other time were there so many women of heroic stature." One could produce a hefty encyclopedia of their names: Jane Addams, Charlotte Perkins Gilman, Lilian Wald, Carrie Chapman Catt, Emma Goldman, Cheryl Eastman, Florence Kelly. But we should not define this "golden age" as a time only for exceptional talents, or for women living in sophisticated metropolitan centers like New York, Boston, Baltimore or San Francisco. It seemed rather to be a salubrious time for women everywhere. Women were enjoying themselves, doing things, even in small-town and rural America. In her book *Ohio Town,* Helen Hooven Santmyer described the original library in her home town of Xenia. It was completely operated and managed by a group of literary women who sustained it out of their own resources: they paid the bills, bought the books, hired the janitor (or more probably swept the snow off the

front steps and carried out the ashes themselves). This is only one of many examples which show that American women, even in the late Victorian age, were not the coddled household ornaments that later mythology has tended to make them. They were active, vivacious and involved; even in small towns, they were seldom left out of whatever important was going on.

So it is not at all true to say that the year 1920 provided a dramatic dividing line between a placid, homebound female on the one hand and some kind of unshackled, devil-may-care creature on the other. The dividing line between the twenties and the period that came just before was not a sharp one, and the women of the twenties were often simply seeking to do the kinds of things that their older sisters, or even their mothers had been doing—but with a bit more drama and gusto. Few women of the twenties could aptly be labeled "revolutionaries." They did not want to wipe out the world they lived in nor did they want to make it over. They simply wanted to enjoy it, more actively and uproariously than their predecessors.

Perhaps this is one of the reasons why the Suffragette movement, so vigorous in the years between 1910 and 1920, petered out immediately after the enactment of the nineteenth amendment. Women wanted the vote, and after that they wanted more of everything that seemed to be available, but with full realization that their goals and potentials were not identical with those of men. By 1920, the prospects for achieving more of women's goals looked good; it was just a matter of getting out and keeping in motion.

Perhaps the decade of the twenties is more

accurately perceived as a cadenza to the golden age that seemed to precede it rather than as the start of something new. But if so, it was also a more complex and intellectually challenging time for women. Flaming youths and flappers there certainly were, but this was merely a gloss on a time when American women were expected to shoulder even more of the nation's cultural life than ever before, for the men were busy not only with commerce, but with the war and its aftermath.

The generation of American men that grew to maturity just before the war, and then were drafted, shot up, and disillusioned by the war's bitter fruits, returned to the mainstream of social life only slowly, and then often with cynical attitudes. Hemingway and other literati belonged to what Gertrude Stein shrewdly called "the lost generation," not a few of whom became expatriates. Others, like Edmund Wilson, returned to America after the war to launch literary careers on this side of the Atlantic, but they were under no illusions that the "Great War" had made the world any safer for democracy, or that the American dream was necessarily worth the kind of horror and death they had seen at the front. Wilson wrote to his friend Stanley Dell in 1921 that the best of America's postwar novels, like Sinclair Lewis's *Main Street,* were written "to tell what a terrible place America is."

During the early twenties, then, many young American males were disaffected, disoriented, depressed. Young women of the same age, however, often appeared to be upbeat, flamboyant and optimistic about the drift of things. There were, it seemed, no exact female counterparts of Hemingway, no books written by women like Edmund

Wilson's and John Peale Bishop's *The Undertaker's Garland,* a doleful evaluation of the emptiness of postwar American society.

While the men who had passed through the war years were often short-circuited, waylaid, women were ready and willing to push forward in earth-shaking ways. This does not mean, of course, that the young women of this period did not feel some of the pangs of cynicism and scepticism. They did—but they also felt the beckonings of new freedom. Where so many men saw the darkness of a world in disarray, its coherence torn apart by the forces of nationalism, greed and dehumanization, women saw something more compelling: their own lights beginning to glimmer, more and more brightly.

The women we meet in this book chose not so much to react to what had happened, during the war and immediately afterwards, as to seize the chance to pursue their own destinies, their own talents. Each of them perceived some new quality of experience in the America of the twentieth century, and set out to analyze, to celebrate, to criticize, even to exploit, a freshly unfolding facet of the cultural experience. They wrote, they flew, they danced, they preached—in short, they *performed* their insights and made public their own experience.

The women profiled in this book are exemplars of the kind of intense and unmediated response to life which was the great genius of the twenties. But they also represent the cost, the difficulty, above all, the *vulnerability* of leaving oneself open to experience. The fate of the nation—caught up in its own expansion and self-discovery, yet unsure of its own values and goals—was the Depression. The women in this book suffered, in varying degrees, a similar fate: psychological exhaustion, alcoholism, illness. Only two of them managed to make it gracefully and productively into old age; the others died young, if not literally, then to some extent spiritually.

But in another sense, they were all survivors. They came through a difficult time with banners flying high. They took extravagant risks with their bodies, hearts and minds, not waiting until things were safe, but forging ahead, often in the face of strong opposition. They maintained highly individual—indeed, eccentric—presences that rank them still among the most memorable women of a century crowded with "famous" people.

Were these women feminists? The answer is surely no, if that term is defined by membership in a purposefully organized program, complete with tracts, programs and professional lobbies. Such "institutionalized" feminism was only beginning to take shape when our heroines were climbing out on their particular limbs, with not much of a safety net except their own talent. Their triumphs, therefore, seem especially thrilling, larger than life. Their failures, too, are big and touching and, for us all, enlightening.

2

Moving Starward

Motion pictures—which quickly came to be called the "movies"—began to capture the American imagination early in the century, and by the nineteen twenties, they were an important part of everyday life for a wide variety of people. Women, especially, were fascinated by the romance and drama of the movies, in part because the "flickers" offered an escape from the rather ordinary and limited world that many of them inhabited. But equally important, the motion picture screen provided American women with an opportunity to see women like themselves having not just jobs, but real careers.

Beginning with D. W. Griffith's delicate heroines, whose fragile features and winsome bodies were displayed to millions in close-up shots, the female face and form came completely to possess the silent screen. The result was a whole new range of possibilities for women to express themselves—profitably—as sexual beings. It can be said, of course, and accurately, that almost from its inception the movie industry exploited women as sexual objects. But on the other hand, it offered women—all kinds of women, not just the rare geniuses—a chance for success. The movies provided a marvelous vehicle for feminine talent, and a potential for fame and riches which had never been available to women. Because the field was so new, there were no rules, no schools; courage, enthusiasm and luck could be enough to turn a shopgirl or a farmer's daughter into a star. Every telephone operator, every beautician could dream, as she read her movie magazines, that she, too, might actually be sharing the silver screen with some handsome leading man.

The silent movies, unlike the stage, required no long period of apprenticeship, and sometimes only the scantiest education or preparation, so young girls of markedly deficient cultural background, like Mabel Normand or Clara Bow, could burst forth on the silent screen and capture audiences everywhere, with talents that were quite real, although untrained. A silent movie star needed, more than any other kind of talent, the ability to project character and meaning *visually,* using nothing more than the face and the body, and these fresh, unselfconscious young women could throw themselves into their roles without the interference of "technique" or "theory." Not a few of these early actresses—Lillian Gish, Mary Pickford, Gloria Swanson—carved immensely successful careers out of very meager materials, often by dint of forceful or even reckless personalities.

Underlying the success of such women was, always,

that elusive quality which Elinor Glyn, author of sultry romance novels, called "It"—"that strange magnetism which attracts both sexes." Glyn gave Hollywood the word it needed to describe that elusive "something special" which separates the stars from the extras, and in 1927, she explained "It" further in a book of the same name. A person possessed of "It," according to Glyn, "must be entirely unselfconscious and full of self-confidence, indifferent to the effect he or she is producing, and uninfluenced by others. There must be physical attraction, but beauty is unnecessary. Conceit or self-consciousness destroys 'It' immediately. In the animal world 'It' demonstrates in tigers and cats—both animals being fascinating and mysterious and quite unbiddable."

The girl who came to personify "It" was, of course, Clara Bow. And Bow's career was almost a perfect symbol of the dreams that the movie business made possible. Clara was born in 1905 into a milieu of absolute poverty, both financial and cultural; she knew little care from her incompetent mother, had only a rudimentary education, and seemed doomed to the depressing life of the Brooklyn streets. But Clara Bow saw something in the movies that gave her hope. The "flickers" were a world of magic, a world of happy endings, especially for the youthful heroines of the movies—all of whom seemed to be trapped, harassed (like Clara Bow herself), only to spring out into the sunlight in the end, each with a handsome and doting hero on her arm.

From the age of ten, Bow was a fanatical movie fan, attending as many shows as she could, subscribing to movie magazines and writing fan letters. At sixteen she entered a contest sponsored by *Motion Picture Classic* magazine, and something about her, something unique, was spotted by the judges; against all odds, Clara won out over the better dressed and more polished competitors. The prize was fit for Cinderella: Clara's picture appeared in the magazine over the hyperbolic caption "the most beautiful girl in the world," and she received an evening gown, a trophy, and a *very* small part in a movie—a part which was, in fact, cut from the final film.

The contest did not make Clara Bow an overnight star, any more than the ball made Cinderalla an instant success, but it was a first step. Her father, a well-meaning and affectionate man who believed emphatically in his daughter, haunted the offices of the movie companies which had not yet moved to the West Coast, telling whoever would listen about Clara. His persistence paid off. Actor-turned-director Elmer Clifton was planning to make a film called *Down to the Sea in Ships,* and he needed a young girl, a gamine typc, to play the part of a stowaway on a whaling ship.

Bow almost didn't get the part, though, because when she turned up to be interviewed, she fitted herself out as a youthful *femme fatale,* not at all the image that had appealed to Clifton in the first place. He waved her aside immediately, saying, "No, no, that's not what we need. I thought you were just a child." But Clara instantly perceived what he wanted. She ripped off her fashionable hat and wiped off the lipstick and rouge, saying "This ain't the real me! I'll show you what I really look like." Clifton was enchanted by the transformation from glamour-puss to teenage moppet, and agreed to give Bow the job—at $50 a week.

The debut in *Down to the Sea in Ships* was a real one this time. Clara did not end up on the cutting room floor; in fact, she enjoyed a major role in the film, much to her surprise. The first time Clara saw the film, the shock of recognizing herself on the screen was so electrifying it left her temporarily speechless. Although she was to see herself on the screen many times afterward, none of these later experiences ever gave her a comparable feeling of ecstasy and triumph. She sat through three performances that day, and her only disappointment came when she stood around in the theater lobby fixing her hair and hoping to be recognized; of course nobody expected to see a movie star in a neighborhood movie palace, and so she wasn't mobbed by fans that day.

But Clara certainly was not the only one to be enchanted by this, her first real screen role. The film reviewer in *Variety* commented that "Clara Bow lingers in the eye after the picture has gone." And the celebrated Robert E. Sherwood (of Algonquin Round Table and *Vanity Fair* fame) went so far as to pronounce Clara's role one of the top performances of 1923. Hollywood, already the movie-making center of the country and hungry for talented teenagers, was obviously just around the corner.

Clara's final movie in New York brought her a role that prefigured the kind of flapper parts with which she would later be identified. The movie, a low budget item, was called *Enemies of Women,* and the only thing going for it was a starring role for Lionel Barrymore. Bow's part was a small one, less significant than her runaway tomboy in *Down to the Sea in Ships,* but it gave her her first opportunity to play a well-made-up and wildly abandoned young woman—*and* she got the chance to dance on a table top. Her dance number proved more memorable in the making than it was in the final film, for it was quickly noted by the crew and those on the set that Clara Bow was dancing this nice little number without any panties on. Even the refined Lionel Barrymore was taken by it all, observing that "You could see all the way to the Virgin Islands."

Clara Bow was not yet eighteen, and already on her way to being the unforgettable incarnation of "It." Soon she was in Hollywood, working for B. P. Schulberg in a small-time company called Preferred Pictures. Clara was not a star, so she worked cheaply, but she had star quality, and when Schulberg moved up in the world—to Paramount Pictures—Clara went too. There she found better scripts, better directors, and a chance to really shine, in films like *Kid Boots, Red Hair, Rough House Rosie,* and *Dancing Mothers*. She had the staunch support of capable leading men like Antonio Moreno, Lane Chandler, James Hall and Warner Baxter, and skilled directors like William Wellman and Victor Fleming. Paramount was soon able to exalt her into the front ranks of the silent sex stars, so that during the late twenties she was every bit the institution that Marilyn Monroe and Brigitte Bardot would be in the 1950s.

Paramount missed no opportunity to build Clara up as a sex goddess—the "wildest jazz baby of them all," the "Brooklyn Bonfire," and most memorably of all, the "It girl." Paramount's resourceful Walter Wanger was so taken with the idea of "It" that he wanted Elinor Glyn to make a novelette out of the idea, calling it "It," of course. Wanger instructed her to sell it to her friend William Randolph Hearst for publication in *Cosmopolitan* and promised to buy

the film rights for fifty thousand dollars. Savvy business woman that she was, Glyn had the novelette on the newsstand in a twinkling, and Paramount immediately announced that the film was already in the works, with (who else?) Clara Bow as the "It" girl. Bow's leading man was to be Antonio Moreno, the only actor of the moment that Miss Glyn had also pronounced to be endowed with "It."

The film that came out of Glyn's little meringue bore scant resemblance to the original, and caused one jaded Hollywood wit to observe that Elinor Glyn was the highest paid writer in the world, having been paid $50,000 for a single word: "It." Dorothy Parker's malicious (and delicious) review of Glyn's book lampooned the author's explanation of the difference between the book and the film:

> Where, I ask you, have I been that no true word of Madame Glyn's literary feats has come to me? But even those far, far better informed than I must work a bit over the opening sentence of Madame Glyn's forward to her novel. "This is *not,* " she says, drawing her emeralds warmly about her, "the story of the moving picture entitled, *It,* but a full character study of the story *It,* which the people in the picture read and discuss." I could go mad, in a nice way, straining to figure that out. But I shall let it stay a mystery.

Parker went on, of course, to demolish the book, silly characters, slight story, and all.

The plot of the movie was as frivolous and tissue-paper thin as that of the book; nonetheless it gave Clara's light a full opportunity to shine. The ambience, of course, was typical of a Clara Bow film. Clara plays a working-class girl whiling away her hours selling lingerie in a large department store. Her girlfriend and working companion points out the new boss to her—"Hot socks, look at that —the new boss." Clara is even more impressed and moves into characteristically swift action: "Sweet Santa Claus, give him to me!" She then plots to meet the debonair Waltham (played by Moreno), first by finagling a date with his comic stooge crony Monty, who is prevailed upon to take her to dinner at the Ritz, where the boss customarily dines. And so on. She wins Waltham's attention immediately and suggests an outing to Coney Island: "Let's go to the beach and do it up right!" Clara Bow, the most fluid and extravagant flirt in film history, melts the stuffed-shirt boss in mere minutes. On the crowded beach she has full leeway to cuddle, kiss, twist about sensuously, reveal her pantalets, and roam her hands through the hero's hair, and up and down his arms.

In all of Hollywood, nobody could do this kind of thing better than Clara Bow. Throughout *It,* Clara is in a constant state of sensual activity, bouncing, blooping, giggling. She commands and demands the whole screen. In her major films with Paramount Clara was blessed with unusually skillful directors, but at the same time she was herself a natural actress who intuitively knew how to play every scene, and invented all of her own visual temptations. There was a kind of perpetual movement about her, a restlessness. Even in alighting from a car her legs were in continuous jazz motion, as if nothing could ever be humdrum or routine.

This dynamic physical presence was certainly part of Clara's power on the screen, but there was something more, too. In 1927, in an interview with *Theater Arts* magazine,

Clara Bow tried to explain what this mysterious thing called "It" was all about, especially in relation to her own gifts and emotional drive.

> The "It" Mme. Glyn attributes to me is something of which I am not aware. As far as I know I think it must be my vivacity, my fearlessness and perhaps the fact that I'm just a regular girl or a tom-girl, one that doesn't think of men much; maybe it's my indifference to them. I really don't care particularly about men. I know four whom I rather like. Each one possesses some one thing that appeals to me—but not one possesses the combination.

Bow's perceptions of her own attractiveness were shrewd ones, and they captured something essential about the transformation of femininity in the twenties. The "new" fashions which women were adopting—bobbed hair, flattened chests, vanishing hips—were all directed toward a "boyish" look. But the reason behind this was not at all a rebellious wish to be unattractive. On the contrary, women believed that throwing away centuries-old impediments of dress would make them *more* appealing to men, would allow them to be right there in the center of things on the golf links or the playing field; the new costumes would show them to be flexible, carefree and ready to go, all traits that the women of the twenties believed would and should be attractive to men.

"It," after all, was not a property of gender. Both men and women could have it; indeed, the primary quality of "It" was defined as a magnetic appeal to *both* sexes. The men of the twenties who achieved movie stardom were somewhat androgynous. When we see the films of screen heros like Ramon Navarro and Rudolph Valentino today, those romantic males seem almost laughably prettified—a far cry from Clint Eastwood and Sylvester Stallone. But like Clara Bow and her "boyish" movie sisters, they projected a tremendous appeal to the audience. The blurring of gender lines became an exciting—in fact, a sexually charged—part of the movie mystique.

Sex and movies. Both enjoyed a sweeping vogue in the twenties, and each was in its own way a new phenomenon. True enough, sex had been around for eons, but for the preceding several decades, people had pretended that it didn't exist. Sex, of course, had not actually been discontinued during the Victorian era; it had only become invisible. The twenties, although commonly perceived as a decade of sexual revolution, when the restraints of prudery were cast aside and Americans began to enjoy a full range of sexual delights, are more accurately described as the time when sex finally came out of the closet. Sex became an item openly discussed, analyzed, admitted and, in some cases, experimented with. Younger Americans certainly did feel freer to express themselves sexually, though it is difficult to say how much of that expressiveness took the form of action and how much of it was mere talk.

But it was not only the young who were making sex fashionable. In sophisticated salons and in elegant hotel dining rooms, older urbanites were talking about the theories of Dr. Freud, whose work had begun to spread through the country like wildfire. There arrived from the continent wholly new words, at first discussed in hushed tones, but shortly bandied about unabashedly at respectable dinner tables: words like "sadism," "masochism," "sublimation,"

"unconscious." The story of Oedipus, previously interesting only to classical scholars, became a fascinating bit of gossip. And "going into analysis" became a popular pastime, as did eager disclosure of the lurid details of one's own sex life and that of others. These topics of conversation, only a decade before, would have been considered bad taste or even blasphemy; they now became routine, trivial.

The movies certainly contributed to the trivialization of sex, just as the new openness about sexuality contributed to the flourishing success of the movies. But as a result of this interaction, the exploitation of women became an integral part of the early movie industry, and developed into a tradition which still persists to some extent today. Although the wide-open industry of the twenties offered incredible possibilities for a few women who "made it," thousands more were at best disappointed and at worst ill-used by Hollywood. Of the hordes arriving daily in the movie capital during the years of glory, only a scant few even received a screen test or an opportunity to put a foot on the first rung of the ladder. Countless of them were waylaid by false promises or were crushed by the immensity of the studio system. Carried along by hope, many became victims of the well-known "casting couch," letting themselves be bamboozled by producers or assistant producers—sometimes even by messenger boys or guards at the front gate who were rumored to have influence.

Even those who succeeded in becoming "movie stars" often failed to survive the experience. Some of the silent screen stars—delicate heroines like Mary Pickford and Lillian Gish as well as savvy types like Gloria Swanson—were tough-minded managers of career and money, who prospered from their Hollywood days. But others, and especially the "sex goddesses," found themselves swiftly eclipsed, with little to show for their days of glory. Many exhausted themselves before the cameras, and suffered from the constant demand to project the energy and gaiety expected from a "star." Clara Bow described her own experience of stardom in 1927:

> I know that everyone looking at me on the screen says: I'll bet she's never unhappy. The truth is that I haven't been happy for many, many months. The person you see on the screen is not my true self at all, it's my screen self. . . .
>
> The public likes me best in wild, fiery roles; those are the roles that take the greatest amount of energy from me, and I can tell you it is not easy. My nerves are at their peak now.

Clara Bow was luckier than some; she continued to work after "talkies" came in, although her parts grew less and less important. But attempts to follow stardom with a "normal" life as a wife and mother were only moderately successful; in time her mental condition deteriorated and she spent the last years of her life coping as best she could with the terrible insomnia which had gripped her since adolescence. Shortly after Clara's first film, her mentally ill mother had been seized with the idea that her daughter's soul would be lost to the "sinful" world of the movies. She awakened Clara in the middle of the night, threatening her wildly with a kitchen knife. From that time on, Clara had difficulty in sleeping, and when death found her in 1965, she was watching the late show on television, trying to get through another wakeful night.

Was this the high cost of movie stardom? Perhaps. But all the same, Clara Bow, who had escaped from the tenements of Brooklyn just on the strength of beauty and vitality, became and remained a legend. She was a symbol of the magic that movies could work—not just for a hundred minutes in the theater, but for a whole life. Whatever her fate was as a star, it was certainly better in many ways than it would have been as a working class wife in Brooklyn.

What made her success possible? What exactly was "It?" In an age when sex was "out of the closet" and into the forefront of conversation and behavior, it was easy to reduce the mysterious "It" to a synonym for sex appeal. In truth, that's probably the way Elinor Glyn basically thought of it. But wittingly or not, Glyn had expressed a more essential and complex phenomenon. "It" was not merely a matter of sex and sexiness. A quality of *character* was also involved, although Glyn might not have put it in just that way. The possessor of "It" was above all a person confidently assured of his or her own personality, without exactly being aware of it. "It" was the tension between cool self-sufficiency and hot energy, a tension that lit up the screen and infused the whole decade of the twenties.

In effect, the movie screen isolated and amplified a special quality of personality which fascinated people in the twenties because it was so much a part of the era itself. "It" was not just to be found in Hollywood; it was everywhere —in the dash and dazzle of the stock market, the naive wickedness of the speakeasies, the new-found speed of the automobile and the airplane. And as that special "It" brand of sexiness became openly part of everyday life, from the provocative new arts to the practical—in more ways than one—zipper, women found themselves suddenly more acceptable, exciting commodities in the marketplace. They could use what had so long been ignored or rejected by society: their own energy and individuality.

Clara Bow, Gloria Swanson, and all the other Hollywood beauties took advantage of this new climate in a simple and obvious way. The women who are about to be introduced in this book followed more complex and subtle routes. But they too were, in their own ways, among the vanguard of women who were moving starward. Although none of them was a "movie star," each was well-known—interviewed, photographed, talked about—during the twenties, and each achieved a degree of fame which lasted long after the jazz age was over. They were among the first American women to become well known *because of their talents and accomplishments,* rather than because of the men they married.

These women of the twenties were, in a very real sense, the first to become what we would call today "successful." As a result, they faced all the difficulties which confront the achievement-oriented women of the eighties, but with no preparation and little help. Yet they also had the rare delight of being the first to reach new ground. How they got there, and how they survived the trip, is revealed (though certainly not explained) in the chapters ahead.

PART TWO

A Magazine of Inventions

3

AIMEE SEMPLE McPHERSON

When H. L. Mencken, the critic-at-large of American life, visited southern California in 1926, he made a point of taking in Aimee Semple McPherson's "show" at the enormous Angelus Temple. Back in Baltimore he described Sister Aimee—the most famous and powerful evangelist in America—to his readers:

> Aimee herself led the choir in a hymn with a lively tune and very saucy words, chiefly aimed at her enemies. Two or three times she launched into very brief addresses. But mostly she simply ran the show. While the quartets bawled and the band played she was busy at a telephone behind the altar or hurling orders in a loud stage whisper at sergeants or corporals on the floor. Obviously, a very managing woman, strongly recalling the madam of a fancy house on a busy Saturday night. A fixed smile stuck to her from first to last.

This account suited the sophisticated Eastern audience, which relished Mencken's well-aimed whacks at the "booboisie." Mencken's *private* views were somewhat different, however. "I sat under Aimee yesterday and had two and a half spells of tumescence," he wrote to his friend Raymond Perl. "Her sex appeal is tremendous." And not only did he find the celebrated lady evangelist overwhelmingly sexy; Mencken, who prided himself on having heard all of the breast beaters and mountebanks of his day—from William Jennings Bryan to Huey Long—declared privately to his friends that Sister Aimee was a genuine spellbinder, that she knew how to get ideas to flow, nay, to march and shout. She had an exquisite sense of timing and dramatic development; she was articulate and eloquent; she knew all of the arts of the spoken word as if she had studied their technique at the foot of some classical orator. Sister Aimee, Mencken admitted, was as different from a back street evangelist as the Parthenon is from a chicken coop.

From the vantage point of the present, Sister Aimee Semple McPherson is distinctly a period piece, floating undisturbed in one of the backwashes of history. Indeed, when she died of an apparent overdose of barbiturates in 1944, she had already been relegated to the national curio chest of misfits and cultural oddities. The International Church of the Foursquare Gospel, which she founded, goes on today without her—and curiously, it has many more churches and members than when the evangelist herself was alive—but it is certainly not in the mainstream of American religious life. Yet even though Sister Aimee's vogue vanished with the time that made it possible, she remains a fascinating figure; books and articles continue to be written

about her, even by people born too late to remember her in the flesh.

Of course much of the vast literature that has grown up around Sister Aimee can be attributed to her colorful and often scandalous personal life, to the uproar and notoriety that seemed to surround all of her doings. No religious figure of American record provided such continuous and pulsating copy for tabloids, gossip columnists and writers of lurid biography. Sister Aimee liked to refer to herself as "the least of all the saints"—a meaningless accolade, perhaps, but one that allowed her to avoid the more obvious honorific just a jot away: the most extravagant of all sinners. Everything about Aimee Semple McPherson was larger than life, and much of it was good. The religious experiences she created for her followers were rich and joy-filled ones; her charities were legion, and she could be personally warm and giving. At the same time, she was shrewd and manipulative, and perhaps even ruthless. Her personal weaknesses and passions always throbbed dangerously near the surface of her ministry. Like many of history's most fascinating figures, Aimee was simultaneously a genius and a charlatan, a sinner *and* a savior.

In spite of all her paradoxes—or perhaps because of them—Aimee was a genuine sensation in the twenties and thirties. No evangelist of today, even with the potent tool of television, has a following that can equal Aimee's for sheer devotion and enthusiasm. How did she do it?

At the height of her popularity, Aimee Semple McPherson preached a sermon on the "Rose of Sharon," and it is said that no one who attended on that occasion has ever been able to forget it. Sister Aimee had been on a long tour of the Orient, and she knew that tens of thousands of her followers would be pushing their way into the Angelus Temple on the day of her return. As she travelled from the East Coast to the West by train, Aimee planned the huge event that would mark her homecoming. She telegraphed her staff that she wanted the temple to be festooned with roses—roses, roses everywhere. The setting for her appearance must, as usual, be appropriate to her theme—and it had to be overwhelming.

So when the great day of Sister's return arrived, her followers found the auditorium one massive bank of roses. Sister's own throne-like chair was completely wreathed with the flowers. Members of the choir wore white robes with red roses pinned over their hearts. Every single one of the 5,400 seats was taken, and many more of the faithful listened over loudspeakers as the band played and the choir sang. Then there was a "Civic Introduction" by the acting mayor of Los Angeles.

Suddenly, as the crowd waited almost breathlessly, a door opened at the back of a huge ramp leading from the balcony to the stage, and down sailed Sister Aimee, tripping, nearly running, long-stemmed American Beauty roses spilling from her arms. From all over the auditorium came cries of "Amen!" and "Hallelujah!" Drums rolled and a xylophone soloist provided a dramatic salute.

All eyes were on Sister, and when it came time for her sermon, she was ready with a powerful emotional

outburst. Every word was memorized, every gesture calculated to bring home some dramatic point. Her theme had come to her, she told her listeners, in India, where she had learned that while a rose only lasts for a few hours, if the attar can be captured and saved, it may last for centuries. She compared Jesus to the Rose of Sharon, saying that only by breaking the rose is the perfume obtained, and so also only the blood of a sacrificial lamb can produce the attar of life everlasting. She tore a petal from a rose and held it up in a spotlight, where it shone like a small drop of blood in her palm.

Sister Aimee brought out the full gamut of emotions in exhorting her followers. She whispered, she bellowed, she chanted, she crooned, she rasped, she pleaded; she was like some giant organ capable of sounding any note from the thinnest reed to thunderous diapasons. Women fainted; many people were so rapt with attention that they fell from their seats. It was a production that even Cecil B. De Mille would have had difficulty matching.

The phenomenon of Aimee Semple McPherson still seems inexplicable. Certainly nothing in Aimee's background could account for her becoming the most powerful American evangelist of the twenties. Sister Aimee came out of the dust—a dense world of elemental cultural poverty—and always seemed to be sinking back into it. She was born Aimee Kennedy in 1890, and she grew up in the forlorn farming community of Ingersoll, Ontario. Her mother, Minnie, had long nourished her own ambitions as a religious spitfire, but at the age of fifteen had been cozened into a bleak and unadventuresome career as the wife of a farmer more than three times her age. Minnie never settled down though; she channeled her energies into the activities of the Salvation Army, rising to the rank of junior Sergeant Major. Another of her outlets was young Aimee's upbringing. Instead of singing lullabies to her baby, Minnie Kennedy crooned hymns; no fairy tales, only Bible stories —Daniel in his den, Jonah and the whale, and all the others. By the time little Aimee was five, she could spout whole chapters from the Bible for fascinated visitors.

Like her mother, Aimee was oversupplied with energies and animal spirits. She was impulsive, hyperactive, directorial even as a small child; fortunately, she was also apparently possessed of a warm and sunny disposition. A natural leader, Aimee excelled at anything that required action, and was both a good student and a good athlete—at least until adolescence. Then, predictably enough, she became very nearly unmanageable. Something which would give her vivacity more scope was needed, and Aimee found it, in the form of Pentecostal religion.

Pentecostals, Aimee discovered, completely outstripped the Salvation Army when it came to purely physical means of expression, to Dionysian flights of emotion, for they "spoke in tongues," went into trances, and rolled and twisted on the floor during their services, thus gaining themselves the disparaging nickname, "Holy Rollers." By the time she was seventeen, Aimee was regularly attending Pentecostal meetings, in spite of her mother's warnings. On one occasion a shocked member of the Salvation Army called upon Mrs. Kennedy to tell her that Aimee was down at the "Holy Rollers' meeting" writhing on the floor and chattering like a monkey. Minnie went down to collect her daughter, but found her still talking in tongues, still in the

middle of some mysterious orgiastic communion with the Holy Spirit.

But even this experience, apparently, did not wholly satisfy Aimee. There was still something missing, some vital element yet needed if she was to know a *full* Christian conversion and to give her life utterly to God. Pentecostals called this missing element "the Baptism of the Holy Spirit," and Aimee was determined to have it. This special baptism is not, however, an ecclesiastical ritual which can be scheduled on a Sunday afternoon and dispatched in a few minutes, Aimee learned. As the Reverend Robert Semple, the young Pentecostal preacher in Ingersoll, explained to her, the Baptism of the Holy Spirit seizes you suddenly, "shakes you from the crown of your head to the corns on your toes. That's what happened on the day of Pentecost and that's what Pentecostalism is all about."

An Irish Protestant from near Belfast, Robert Semple had emigrated from Northern Ireland to the United States at the age of seventeen. The Holy Spirit had gripped him, he told Aimee, while he was working in Chicago, where he sold Irish linen at Marshall Field's. One evening he had been out walking, and as he passed the open door of a noisy revival meeting, he had almost instantaneously felt the Spirit jolt him from head to foot. Laying aside his plans and his job at Field's, Robert set off as an itinerant preacher of the gospel.

When Aimee met him in Ingersoll, Semple had been preaching in small Canadian towns for about a year. Wildly impressed by him, she made a point of getting away from the Kennedy farm and into Ingersoll as frequently as possible, in spite of Minnie's exhortations and threats. On one occasion Aimee found herself snowbound and, unable to return home, she stayed with Sister Barrett, a leading Pentecostal who regularly provided lodging for the Reverend Semple. Throughout that day and much of the night, Aimee prayed for the Baptism of the Holy Spirit. Toward dawn she began whispering "Glory to Jesus," repeating the phrase over and over until it seemed to become an involuntary reflex welling up from deep inside her. After a time, "Glory to Jesus" was replaced by unintelligible babbling.

Robert Semple was awakened by Aimee's ecstatic utterances, and rushing downstairs he joined her in thanking God for the "miracle." "You've changed my life," Aimee told him, and before long she was kissing him, the Spirit's passion having turned for the moment into a more recognizable human emotion.

Predictably enough, Aimee and Robert Semple soon announced their plans to marry and to go to China as missionaries. Exactly how they hoped to disseminate the Pentecostal brand of Christianity among the Chinese was not at all clear, but these are not the sorts of questions asked by youth. In any case, Aimee and Robert shortly swept out of sight, bound for the Orient, with Mother Minnie convinced she would never see her child again.

Alas, this phase of Aimee's life was to be short-lived. In a little more than a year Robert Semple was dead; he had, however, provided his teenage bride with a daughter, who was named Roberta Star Semple. Aimee cabled for help to Minnie, who sent money for the young mother and baby to get home. From this point on, Aimee and her mother would be linked together fatefully for the rest of their lives, partly to their mutual benefit, mostly to their mutual discomfort.

Before long, Aimee married a second time, gaining the rest of her impressive name from Harold McPherson, a decent but wholly uninteresting grocery clerk. They quickly had a son, but Aimee did not settle comfortably into ordinary life. She was painfully depressed, beset by vague religious yearnings which seemed to have no purpose. Inconsolable, Aimee considered suicide—and threatened to take her hapless husband with her. Then suddenly, everything changed: Aimee Semple McPherson heard the Call. She was feverishly determined to spread the gospel, and when she couldn't persuade Harold—who emphatically had *not* heard the Call—to join her in a life of itinerant preaching, Aimee simply took herself and the two children back to Canada, where before long she was being invited to preach in the small towns around Ingersoll.

From the very outset Aimee's preaching style was distinctive, and remarkably effective. She didn't simply "take" the platform, she ran to it like a winged messenger, catching the congregation off-guard and stirring interest right from the start. "Oh, *hallelujah*!" she would begin, "I have prayed for *you*, Oh, how I have *stormed* the gates of *heaven* beseeching the Lord! 'O Father, give me *souls* for my hire,' I prayed. 'Bring them in from the highways and byways to hear Thy precious *Word*.' "

Aimee's voice would rise and fall in mesmerizing cadences. She whispered. She shouted. She told stories from her childhood in hushed, intimate tones, as though each individual in the congregation were her only partner in the conversation. And she used the plain speech of ordinary life, embellished, naturally, with sonorous phrases from the King James Bible. She joked with her audience, giving them the feeling that each of them was on intimate terms with her:

"You know, I'm just a helpless woman, folks. I ain't got me no bag of tricks. When Jesus wanted a crowd, all He had to do was walk on water. Well, I swim pretty good, but I haven't got that walking on water business yet. Besides, even if I *could* do it, you don't have any water in these parts to walk on!"

Already in 1915, Aimee Semple McPherson had developed a manner and style guaranteed to arouse believers. Interestingly, she did not threaten punishment or hellfire; she promised relief, comfort, assurance and joy to anyone who would respond to the Call and "follow Jesus." This happy message, energetically delivered by an attractive young woman, drew audiences wherever Aimee went. For a while Harold McPherson joined her in her evangelical travels. (He can be seen in photographs of this period uneasily clutching a Bible that had been thrust into his hands, looking as if he were about to be unceremoniously yanked off to the railroad depot to depart for some new revivalistic frenzy in the hinterlands.) But by 1917, he had had enough of the missionary life, and what he described in an interview years later as his wife's "wildcat habits" and "dual personality." Aimee and Harold separated for good.

These years were grim ones for Aimee Semple McPherson, as she lived the dreary life of an aspiring but only marginally successful tent evangelist. It was a world of mud and rain, of deserted fairgrounds in one-horse towns, of tents that wouldn't stay up, of volunteers who would walk away with the day's profits, of contemptuous glances from traditional churchgoers and hostile local clergy. It was scanty meals cooked on a smelly oil stove and eaten off boxes or crates. It was a life that none but the most

foolhardy female would have endured. Still, Aimee kept the show on the road, cruising the eastern half of Canada and the United States in the Gospel Auto (a 1912 Packard), and slowly but surely, she improved her act.

Los Angeles in 1918 was basically middle class and middling minded, devoid of any real glamour. Whatever glamour would shortly be provided by the nearby movie colony was to be closely held, not spread to the retired Iowa farmers, quick-profit real estate speculators, tradesmen and small-plot garden farmers who made up the preponderance of the citizenry. The Los Angeles of this period was perfectly described by novelist Saul Bellow in his novel *Seize the Day*: "In Los Angeles all the loose objects in the country were collected, as if America tilted and everything that wasn't tightly screwed down had slid into southern California." The churches of the region especially did not seem to be prepared for this deluge. Most of them were bland, traditional, tepid. The city needed someone to whoop it up for the plain folk, and that someone now arrived. Aimee Semple McPherson had heard a new Call, the siren song of California.

Sister Aimee began her ministry in Los Angeles one week after her arrival in the city. The place was a dingy upstairs meeting room in the Victoria Hall Mission at 125 South Spring Street. There, Pastor Jacobs, a bald, burly man in his fifties, warned Aimee that the city was a haven for fakes and "false prophets." "Cultists in this town," Jacobs admonished her, "preach salvation through everything from weight-lifting to orgies of the flesh— it's unthinkable, abysmal. One imposter teaches mind reading as the road to God. We've got the temperance crowd, the brain-breathing cult, the evangelical atheists. Why, they've even invaded our own true faith. . . . "

But Aimee knew by instinct that this was the place to put down her roots. In only four months she had enough converts and loyal followers that she, Minnie and the children were able to move into a real home—a two-story bungalow on Orange Grove Drive. The lot, the materials, and all the labor for this house had been provided by her newly found disciples. Aimee called it "the house that God built."

Meanwhile, she set about the business of becoming famous in Los Angeles. First, she informed Pastor Jacobs that she intended to employ musicians in her services at the Victoria Hall Mission. Jacobs was horrified, but word got around the city, and soon fair-sized crowds began coming to hear the "Christian Orchestra." Within a week, the one-thousand-seat auditorium at Victoria Hall was filled to capacity every night. That being the case, Minnie made arrangements to rent the Los Angeles Philharmonic Auditorium, the city's largest, with seats for 3,500. There Aimee suspended a gigantic banner eight feet high and fifty feet long, which declared:

AIMEE SEMPLE MCPHERSON—LADY EVANGELIST
NIGHTLY 7:30 P.M. FULL ORCHESTRA, CHOIR
HOLY GHOST REVIVAL

And soon this space too was filled to capacity.

What did Aimee have to say that gripped the

people of Los Angeles so mightily? Basically, the same things she had been saying in small Canadian towns and in camp-meetings throughout the United States since 1915. She preached God's blessings, His healing power and the gifts of the Spirit for those who sincerely turn to Jesus. Pathetically simple, perhaps, but people were evidently hungry to hear it—and to see it, for Aimee's L.A. services were spectacularly colorful. "Oh, what a *blessing* we've had here," she would intone. "And it's not my doing—oh no! I'm just a little woman, God's handmaiden, the least of all the saints." And the crowd would go crazy.

Not everyone—and particularly not the pastors of the more established Los Angeles churches—approved of Sister Aimee, but if this bothered her, she didn't show it much or often. After a high-profile trip to the East Coast "to drive the Devil from New York," Aimee became widely known throughout the country and her following in California seemed to increase almost exponentially. By then it was clear that her evangelistic campaigns needed a permanent home-base, a real *church*. And so she created one: the "Foursquare Gospel Church." The term "Foursquare" referred to the four basic tenets which Sister Aimee claimed were revealed to her in a vision: Regeneration, Divine Healing, the Second Coming of Christ and the Baptism of the Holy Ghost.

The religion was a typical fundamentalist sect of the kind that was very familiar in the 1920s, in which the Bible was held to be the absolute and literal Word of God. But Aimee's revival offered more than any of the others. There was speaking in unknown tongues and interpretation of them (Sister Aimee was one of a number of revivalists in the twenties who claimed the ability to speak and interpret such languages as Aramaic, Coptic, Ancient Hebrew, and others, although there is no evidence that she ever studied any of these languages); there were Spirit Baptism, divine healing, and the performance of other miracles; there was belief in the imminent second coming of Christ, including "the Rapture"; there was a final judgment very literally interpreted, which scenario included an actual hell of fire and brimstone into which sinners would be cast, and an actual heaven of indescribable bliss for true believers.

Of course what really held all these ideas together was the personality of Aimee Semple McPherson herself. Her sect was thoroughly charismatic, with total focus on the divine and supernatural powers of the leader. But the Church of the Foursquare Gospel was also plastic and eclectic—things went in and out of fashion through the years. Some elements Sister Aimee had taken over from the Salvation Army; she loved bands, horns, huge choirs and loud organs, all of which would have been spurned by many other fundamentalist churches of the twenties. There was no standard or prescribed format for the services in Sister Aimee's meetings, because she always reached out for things that would appeal and which she could use to dramatic advantage. If she was getting any mileage out of performing miracles (and she frequently did), she'd perform miracles; if she got publicity out of doing good works for the poor she'd take herself into some downtrodden neighborhood and distribute food to the hungry. What worked was allowed to stay; what didn't work was cast out.

Under Aimee's leadership the Church of the

Foursquare Gospel was a joyous one-ring circus, and by 1922—only four years after she arrived in Los Angeles—a fabulous "circus tent" was under construction. When the Angelus Temple was completed, it looked like a glorified skating rink from the outside; the inside was, like Aimee herself, cheerfully gaudy. Clustered above the temple's main doors—"crystal ones," as she had insisted—were draped American flags. The temple was much like a theater, with dozens of semicircular rows of seats, two vast balconies and a large baptismal pool flanked by heavy curtains. The seats dropped in tiers to a sizeable orchestra pit and stage, which was framed by an elaborately carved plaque that read: JESUS CHRIST, THE SAME YESTERDAY, AND TODAY, AND FOREVER. As the audience sat in the temple, they gazed up at the great organ's thirty-foot-high gold facade and at the mural of Christ with hands outstretched, "one toward heaven, the other toward Aimee."

Aimee pulled out all the stops for a dedication service in the new temple on New Year's Day, 1923. In honor of the occasion she exchanged her usual nurse's uniform—which had emphasized her matronly qualities—for a white silk gown. An American Beauty rose, matching the color of her lipstick, was pinned in her hair. Although her audience may not have realized it, Sister Aimee was beginning the transformation from mere evangelist into goddess. She had arrived in Los Angeles a slightly plump, rather maternal brunette; by the end of the twenties, she would be a svelte blonde whose sexual magnetism was not the least weapon in her evangelical arsenal.

Always theatrical, Sister Aimee became more and

more dramatic as her successes grew. A *Los Angeles Times* reporter described the scene at the Angelus Temple in this way:

> Every tiny item on the program of her service is palpitating with drama. Dramatically, picturesquely, Sister Aimee became entangled in the festooning ribbons as she proceeded down the runway, as the spotlight followed her, and the other lights illuminated the stained glass windows depicting the life of Christ. She waved like a happy joyous girl as the crowd applauded and cheered and seemed about to dance for sheer joy.

Sister's services were always filled with motion and with representations of one sort or another. Aimee invented and perfected the technique of "illustrated sermons," using skits, tableaux, and pantomimes, fully enhanced by footlights, scenery, props and other elements from the theater. Sister Aimee especially loved costumes—however extravagant, however far-fetched. Once after she had been stopped for speeding and given a ticket, Aimee came on the platform in a motorcycle, dressed in full police uniform, with cap, and preached a sermon entitled, "Stop! You are Breaking God's Law!"

All this was not merely hype; the scenes, props and costumes employed at the Angelus Temple helped Aimee to make her ideas clear and vivid to a populace generally as undergifted in imagination as Sister herself was gifted. Since her followers were enjoined against attending the theater and the movies (yes, in the film capital of the world), they were always starved for drama in their lives, and Sister provided it. She gave them every bit as good a show—

sometimes better—than the movie palaces, and no one ever doubted he was getting his money's worth.

Sometimes, however, Sister Aimee's dramatic ideas became too flamboyant and had finally to be reeled in by common sense. At one point in her career, when she was hoping to spread her faith across the ocean and around the world, her overeager imagination latched on to the idea of calling her church a "Salvation Navy," with naval uniforms for herself and her entourage. Sister Aimee would be the Admiral, and all the officials of the church would hold lesser ranks. Even the lowliest choirboy would wear a middy's uniform. The idea eventually had to be scuttled, however, when Aimee's tireless factotums and functionaries got to squabbling about their ranks. Nevertheless, traces of this grand scheme remain, for the mission churches of the Four-square Gospel Church are still called "lighthouses" and many carry out that theme in their architecture.

Aimee's dramatic flair, along with the exuberant sexuality she developed and projected, brought her a great many converts—and, inevitably, plenty of detractors as well. The most fervent of her critics, having simmered helplessly for years while Aimee took Los Angeles by storm, were only too pleased and eager when she finally seemed to run aground. The famous "kidnapping" of Aimee Semple McPherson—which was very likely in fact a cover-up for a romantic escapade—had all the makings of a huge scandal. For a while, it looked as if it would, indeed, topple the mighty Mrs. McPherson.

The whole thing began when Aimee decided to build her own radio station, and hired Kenneth Ormiston to construct and manage it. He quickly had KFSG (Kalling

FourSquare Gospel) on the air, and Sister Aimee's message could be heard all over the western United States by 1924. But in spite of his efficiency, Ormiston was fired toward the end of 1925, at the insistence of Aimee's mother, who always kept a tight rein on the Church's business. Minnie may well have suspected some romantic involvement between Aimee and the already-married Ormiston, and although celibacy was not one of the cornerstones of the foursquare gospel, Sister Aimee as the focus of the whole movement had to be above reproach.

Not long after Ormiston's firing, Aimee left on a pilgrimage to the Holy Land. She returned on April 24, 1926, rested and triumphant, only to disappear—the victim, it seemed, of drowning—less than a month later (May 18). Her followers were desolate, and the search for Aimee, or her body, was intense; in fact, two men drowned while trying to recover the presumed body. Then suddenly, on June 23, Aimee Semple McPherson turned up in a hospital in the small town of Douglas, Arizona, recuperating from the effects of her alleged "kidnapping."

What really happened? Aimee's own story was that a strange woman named Rose had led her from the beach where she was swimming near Ocean View Hotel in Los Angeles, to a car where a dying infant supposedly lay in need of prayers. Arriving at the car, Aimee said she was met by another stranger, who knocked her unconscious with a drug-saturated cloth. She was then abducted to a small two-story house, forced to write a letter to Minnie demanding $500,000 ransom, and later taken to a shack in what "proved" to be Mexico's Sonora Desert. From there, Aimee claimed, she had managed to escape her kidnappers and to

make her way on foot across grueling stretches of desert until she reached Douglas, where she found help and was admitted to the hospital.

Aimee's kidnapping story made the whole affair a matter for police investigation, and the fact that two lives had been lost in the search for her brought her tale under even more intense scrutiny. Soon, the press noticed some rather unusual points in Aimee's version of the events. One reporter was amazed, for instance, at how thoughtful her "kidnappers" were to provide her with a corset in exactly her size and style, and from a department store where she had a charge account. (Aimee was wearing this garment when she arrived at the hospital in Douglas, though she had been "kidnapped" wearing a bathing suit.)

At the time of Aimee's disappearance, Robert Shuler, a rival evangelist, was head of the Church Federation of Los Angeles, from which Aimee herself had resigned some two years earlier. Following the events of May-June, 1926, Shuler began packing in the crowds at his Trinity Church by preaching on the McPherson case. Largely at his instigation, the Church Federation issued a statement which read, in part:

> Be it resolved:
>
> First, that the executive committee of the Church Federation of Los Angeles declare itself absolutely neutral as regards the supposed and reported differences of opinion that may exist between Mrs. McPherson and those whom she terms her "enemies;"
>
> Second, that we solemnly confirm that the district attorney, the sheriff, the police department and the grand jury as impaneled in Los Angeles County should make an honest, sincere and thoroughly ade-

> quate investigation of this whole matter, without fear or favor, and report to the people their findings. . . .

Los Angeles District Attorney Asa Keyes was probably as dismayed by this statement as were Minnie Kennedy and Aimee McPherson. Quite certainly, Aimee had her enemies, and they were not all imaginary ones. A growing number of Los Angeles's pastors were chagrined at losing so many from their own congregations to the Angelus Temple (to say nothing of the loss of income this exodus caused). At the same time, however, Aimee was a kind of folk-heroine. She had campaigned ceaselessly on behalf of every conceivable charity, had worked for pay raises for city employees, and had contributed thousands of dollars to the poor. Keyes would have had a hard time proving that Aimee's life and work were pernicious, and he was liable to lose his own position if he pressed the investigation too vigorously.

By this time, however, the suspicions which had been aroused had taken form, and the scenario suggested was a racy one. It was widely theorized that Aimee's "pilgrimage" had in fact been a tryst with Kenneth Ormiston in Italy, and that the "kidnapping" was a cover-up for a second romantic adventure, this time in Carmel. The titillating possibilities of this version spurred on Aimee's enemies, and it soon became obvious that a public hearing of some sort could not be avoided.

So on the morning of July 8, 1926, Aimee, attended by a phalanx of Temple escorts and attired in a simple white crepe dress and a long blue cape, made her way downtown to the massive Hall of Justice, in answer to a summons from the

grand jury. At this hearing, District Attorney Keyes not only probed every inconsistency in Aimee's story—and there were many—but also raised questions concerning Kenneth Ormiston, for at least one witness had reported seeing McPherson and Ormiston in a car together a day before Aimee reappeared in Douglas, Arizona. Through it all, Aimee cheerfully maintained her story of kidnapping, and later that afternoon she made her own summation to the seventeen men and two women of the jury, defending her ministry and explaining its humble origins in moving detail.

"I bought a little tent," Aimee told them, "a poor little tent very full of holes, and from that I saved my money and bought a bigger one, and that has been the story. I drove my own stakes, patched the tent, tied the guide ropes almost like a man. . . . Then came the building of the Angelus Temple. I came here and got a vacant piece of land and hired horses and scrapers and bossed the men myself and went out to build a foundation with my little capital. . . . I have never put my money in oil wells or ranches or even clothes or luxuries. My great thought has always been —and this can be absolutely proved—for the service of the Lord and my dear people."

Her voice ringing throughout the courtroom, Aimee categorically denied allegations that she had invented the kidnapping story as a publicity stunt, or that she had fallen in love and had gone off to have an abortion. "I would rather never have been *born* than to have caused this blow to God's *Word* and His *work*! I had rather I had never seen the light of day when the name of Jesus Christ, whom I love, should be *crucified* and people say, 'There is Sister. She has been preaching, and if her story is wrong—!' "

Some of the jury members began weeping as Aimee asked them to consider not only her own good name, but the welfare of her children.

Later that week, though, Aimee's defense suffered a serious setback when documents analyst Milton Carlson testified that the "ransom note" sent by the "kidnappers" was in his opinion a forgery. "It's too long for kidnappers who mean business," he said, "and it's preoccupied with ridiculously detailed and unnecessary descriptions of how the crime was perpetrated." By the middle of July more damaging testimony was heard. Charles Pope, an automobile dealer from Tucson, positively identified Aimee as the woman he had seen standing in front of the Club International in Agua Prieta some three weeks before her alleged "escape" from the desert.

On July 20, 1926, the grand jury released its report, declaring that "in the alleged kidnapping of Aimee Semple McPherson . . . there is insufficient evidence to warrant an indictment against alleged kidnappers."

The case did not end there, however, not by any means. Neither the press nor Aimee's rivals intended to let the matter die quietly, and Aimee was vulnerable to all sorts of legal charges if the affair could be proven a hoax which had cost the lives of two young men. So it seemed a real miracle when a "Mrs. Lorraine Wiseman" appeared, looking astonishingly like Sister Aimee, and announcing that she was the identical twin of the woman who had *really* been with Kenneth Ormiston in Carmel! (The twin sister, married and the mother of three children, was reluctant to come forward herself, according to Lorraine.)

The newspapers, understandably, were sceptical,

though they found Lorraine a very willing source. She virtually camped out at their offices, babbling her story repeatedly and insisting that she could not rest until she saw Mrs. McPherson vindicated. Soon, however, investigative reporters had discovered that Mrs. Wiseman was wanted in several cities in California for cashing bogus checks, and that during the two weeks she supposedly spent in Carmel, she was actually in Los Angeles working as a seamstress. To make matters worse for McPherson, police detectives who apprehended Lorraine discovered in her purse a packet of photographs in which she and Aimee had posed wearing identical dresses and hairstyles. Mrs. Wiseman was arrested on the bad check charges; Aimee, meanwhile, expressed total surprise at the turn of events.

After her arrest, Mrs. Wiseman confessed that she had been approached in San Francisco on July 30 by a complete stranger who told her she would be handsomely rewarded if she were willing to go to L.A. to help vindicate Aimee Semple McPherson. Lorraine charged, further, that Minnie Kennedy had promised her $5,000 cash if she agreed to testify she had been in Carmel with Ormiston. Finally, Lorraine produced the "affidavit of Mrs. X" (supposedly sworn by the "twin sister") written in Aimee's own hand.

Sister Aimee once remarked that if she pulled out a gun and shot someone dead in full view of her congregation, the majority of her followers would still believe in her. Apparently there was some truth in this, for throughout the kidnapping scandal, Aimee's Temple members remained faithful. When, shortly after Mrs. Wiseman's arrest, Aimee told her congregation that she herself might soon be arrested, she was greeted with cheers and shouts of "God bless you,

Sister!" In the presence of her followers, Aimee dropped to her knees, saying:

> One day I will meet my God in heaven, along with my friends and all my loyal followers and my beloved husband, Robert Semple. And as I expect to meet my God, *my story is as true as it was the first time I told it.*

All the same, Aimee was indicted on felony charges and a lengthy pretrial hearing ensued. After 3,600 pages of evidence had been recorded, Aimee and her mother were both bound over for trial on counts that would carry maximum sentences of forty-two years in prison. But Aimee had not been idle all this time, and her preparations for this eventuality had included hiring detectives to get damaging information against District Attorney Keyes. Aimee had declared full-scale war against Keyes from her pulpit, and her accusations concerning Keyes's diversion of a "secret fund" intended for the prosecution of thieves and murderers to the case against McPherson (and possibly, to his own bank account) were enough to bring Keyes under investigation.

So perhaps it is not too surprising that, on the day Aimee's trial was scheduled to begin, District Attorney Keyes appeared in court and, without preamble, asked that all charges against McPherson and her mother be dropped, stating that testimony already given should enable McPherson "to be judged in the only court of her jurisdiction—the court of public opinion." Charges against Kenneth Ormiston were eventually dismissed, and even Mrs. Wiseman was freed. Ironically, Asa Keyes was the only one who went to jail; he was found guilty of accepting bribes on several

occasions and spent nineteen months in San Quentin Prison.

Aimee's trial was as severe a test as her charismatic power could be subjected to—and she passed with flying colors. For ten more years, she continued at a sustained peak of popularity. The sophisticated set ridiculed her, of course, but they couldn't ignore her. When Aimee's autobiography, *In the Service of the King*, was published in 1928, Dorothy Parker was unable to resist reviewing it, and her scathing comments revealed the essential garishness and simplemindedness which were obvious to anyone who looked at Aimee's style closely. "She writes," the reviewer said, "as many other three-named authoresses have written before. Her manner takes on the thick bloom of rich red plush. The sun becomes 'that round orb of day' (as opposed, I expect, to those square orbs you see about so much lately); maple syrup is 'Springtide's liquid love gift from the heart of the maple wood'; the forest, by a stroke of inspiration, turns out to be 'a cathedral of stately grandeur and never ceasing wonder and awe'. . . . the ocean—you'll never guess—is 'a broad expanse of sparkling silver'. . . . "

Aimee's writing reflected her preaching—both were often trite and sometimes trashy. But when Aimee *preached*, nothing seemed to matter but the experience she created around her. And the 1920s was a time hungry for experience, eagerly willing to accept whatever scenario of joy and prosperity seemed most persuasive. Aimee's "theology" fit in perfectly with the relentless optimism of the twenties, for it emphasized joy and light, high spirits and success. There was no mourner's bench at Angelus Temple, no wailing over sins, no long lectures on hell and damnation. Dark shadows were occasionally allowed to dart in, but Sister Aimee could always chase them away, and that was her great power.

The success of Aimee Semple McPherson is difficult to explain to anyone who only reads about it in books. To those who were exposed to it, and fell under the spell of the great angel herself, Aimee's overwhelming career seems not at all strange. One of those captivated witnesses was actor Anthony Quinn, who wrote about Aimee in his autobiography *The Original Sin*. Raised a Roman Catholic, Quinn attended Angelus Temple as a teenager because some Temple members had prayed for his sick grandmother, and she had recovered. Quinn remembers the Temple as a warm and generous place; above all, though, he remembers Sister Aimee. "I was fourteen when I met the most magnetic personality I was ever to encounter. Years later, when I saw the great actresses at work I would compare them to her. As magnificent as I could find Anna Magnani, Ingrid Bergman, Laurette Taylor, Katherine Hepburn, Greta Garbo and Ethel Barrymore, they all fell short of that first electric shock Aimee Semple McPherson produced in me."

"Electrifying" is a word that can be applied to only a few actresses, and to still fewer of those who write and stage-manage their own material. Aimee was one of the great actress/producers of her day—that, in a city of screenwriters, directors, and stars. Her culture may have been thin, her theology confusing, but when Sister herself arose, none of these things seemed to matter. She could bring the house down with a simple wave of her arm.

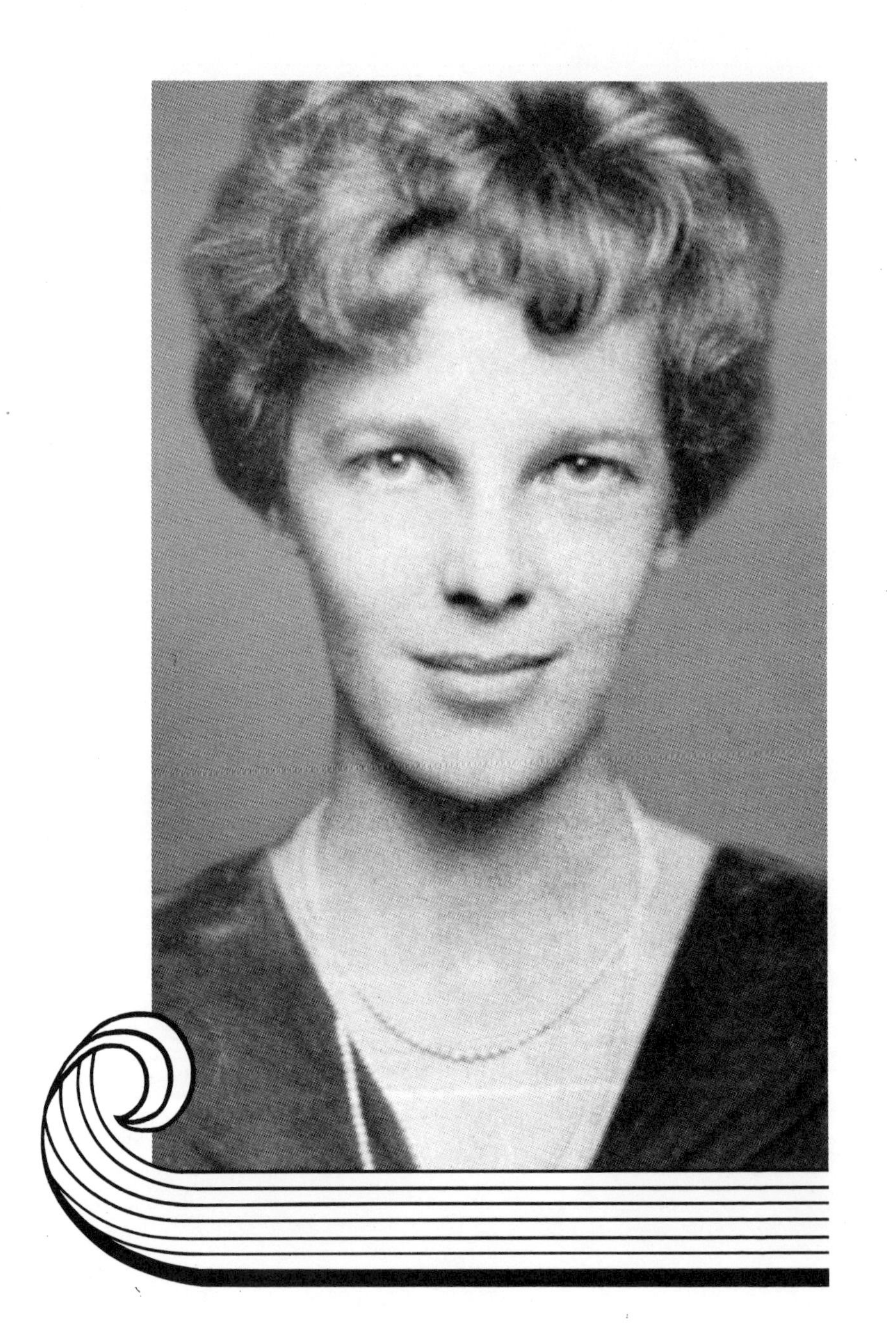

4

AMELIA EARHART

SUCCESS WAS ENTIRELY DUE GREAT SKILL OF MR. STULTZ STOP HE WAS ONLY ONE MILE OFF COURSE AT VALENTIA AFTER FLYING BLIND FOR TWO THOUSAND TWO HUNDRED AND FORTY SIX MILES AT AVERAGE SPEED OF ONE HUNDRED THIRTEEN MPH.

This cable was Amelia Earhart's answer to President Calvin Coolidge, who had sent a message of congratulations to her on becoming, in 1928, the "first woman to fly across the Atlantic." Earhart was perfectly aware of the truth about her achievement; what she had actually become was the first woman to *ride* in a plane flown across the Atlantic by a man. She had no illusions about her accomplishment and didn't try to sell any illusions to the rest of the world. But at the same time, Earhart didn't mind people thinking of her as "Lady Lindy" because she knew that in a few years she would make their fantasy come true by completing the first woman's *solo* transatlantic flight.

The tone of her telegram to Coolidge captures almost perfectly the character of Amelia Earhart: independent, cool, and above all, fascinated with flying. Her love affair with the sky started at her first sight of an airplane, and was still a compelling romance when she left on her last and longest flight in 1937. Earhart's career in aviation covered nearly twenty years, and during that time, although she was certainly not the only—and not even the best—woman pilot, she became a symbol of the new possibilities which the age of flight seemed to be opening up for women.

In everything she did, both professionally and personally, Earhart was focused and determined. Her sights were always clearly set, and she approached every project with a no-nonsense attitude, accepting the risks, prepared for failure, but planning on success. She wrote clearly and with a certain degree of charm; she stood up forthrightly for the principles she believed in; she was a loyal daughter, sister, and wife. (The last of these roles, however, she accepted *very* reluctantly.) In short, Amelia Earhart was a woman who neither let herself be controlled by convention nor felt herself driven to flaunt it. She simply went her own way.

For all these reasons, Amelia Earhart's story is not a very *dramatic* one. She doesn't seem to have felt much inner conflict, and she didn't involve herself a great deal in the kind of "society" which generates excitement. To be sure, she was the object of gossip, but her air of indefatigable common sense seemed to dissipate scandal. There were many pressures on her too—pressure to master the new and

increasingly complicated field of aviation while under the super-watchful eyes of the press and public; pressure to prove that a woman was equal to the challenges of flying; pressure to meet hundreds of deadlines, in the air and on the ground. But she claimed to take it all in stride, and there is no evidence to the contrary.

The story of Amelia Earhart's life apparently unfolded almost like a very modern-day fairy tale, right up to its ambiguous ending. So it would be easy to say "what a lucky girl" or "what a pretty story" and leave it at that. But still . . . what was it about the times and the woman which made this unusual story possible?

In 1928, Amelia Earhart was teaching English at a settlement house in Boston. Captain H. H. Riley called her at Denison House in April of that year, and, as Earhart recalled in her memoir *The Fun of It*, he asked "if I should be interested in doing something for aviation which might be hazardous." Having accepted the risks of flying years before, when she had begun her pilot's training, Amelia had no trouble deciding on her answer. It was yes.

Actually, the original plan for the first transatlantic flight by a woman had called for the passenger to be a wealthy lady, Mrs. Fredrick Guest (the former Amy Phipps), who had acquired the Fokker *Friendship* for the purpose of being flown to Europe by professional pilots. Unfortunately, Mrs. Guest had to back down from this derring-do because her family put up a fuss about the project and steadfastly refused to let her go. But while she had given way herself, she was still insistent that some American girl should fly the Atlantic, already conquered by male aviators a number of times since 1919. Some friends recommended Earhart, and people were sent out to interview her in Boston and find out if she were suitable. Earhart loved the idea, but she had no clue as to what she would say to the interviewers, how she could convince them she was right for the job. "I was interviewed," she later wrote, "by David T. Layman, Jr., and John S. Phipps, and found myself in a curious situation. If they did not like me at all, or found me wanting in too many respects, I would be deprived of the trip. If they liked me too well, they might be loathe to drown me. It was therefore necessary for me to maintain an attitude of impenetrable mediocrity. Apparently I did because I was chosen."

Amelia certainly had an impenetrable quality, something that never left her, but it was never one of mediocrity. She must have impressed her examiners, though, as she did so many people afterward, as a reliable but somewhat abstract and far-off female, a kind of blank tablet on which things were always waiting to be written. She was above all a solid, capable airplane pilot who could, if necessary, make her terms at Davey Jones's locker.

But there were other considerations besides Earhart's talent and enthusiasm for aviation. Among the backers of the transatlantic flight were Paramount Pictures and publisher George Putnam. Part of the deal made with Amelia involved her promise to write a book, as well as a number of newspaper articles, about her experience as the first woman to cross the Atlantic by plane. A cross-country series of personal appearances by Earhart was also planned for the

months following her return from Europe. The entire venture, it appears, had been conceived of as a major media event with, Putnam explained to Amelia, "instant celebrity" as her reward for undertaking the hazardous flight.

The extreme attractiveness of this offer from Paramount and Putnam must certainly have appealed to Amelia's ambitions. By April of 1928 she was, after all, no babe in the woods. She was thirty years old, had been flying planes for eight years, owned her own Kinner aircraft, had been licensed by the *Fédération Aéronautique*, and was a competent writer. Besides, a lack of self-confidence had never been one of Earhart's problems. She was supremely comfortable with the challenges of air travel and quite unafraid of attempting the new and the hazardous. The proposal offered a chance to focus her life, to find international recognition and, perhaps, some degree of financial security for herself and her family.

The flight and its purpose—to carry a woman across the Atlantic—were kept secret as long as possible. But bad weather over the Atlantic in 1928 caused a number of false starts, and word got out that such a trip was in the offing. (The same thing had happened to Lindberg the year before.) While the project was struggling to get "off the ground," the name of Amelia Earhart came to the attention of the public. Even Earhart's mother and sister became aware of her adventure only on reading about it in the newspapers after one of those false starts when the weather was fine at home and grim out over the ocean.

The Fokker C-2 that was to make the flight was also part of a much larger and more important aviation project: the plane was scheduled to be used by Commander

Richard E. Byrd on his forthcoming flight to Antarctica. Wilmer Stultz, the pilot, and Louis Gordon, the mechanic, were members of the Byrd team, and Amelia spent more time hearing about the preparations for Antarctica than she did about the trip to Europe —which never seemed to come off, as the weeks of May 1928 dragged by with little or no improvement in the weather.

Finally the team got away from Boston, only to find themselves holed up in Newfoundland for another wearisome two weeks, during which Earhart found herself, for the first time in her life, pestered by members of the press. Of course this proved to be only a foretaste of the celebrity status which would shape the rest of her life. The two male members of the flight team took the tedium of waiting rather hard, and Stultz, apparently a drinking man, spent a good deal of his time in the local pub. Earhart, a non-drinking woman, was sufficiently upset with the whole situation that she played with the idea of wiring back to the United States for a backup pilot. In the end, however, she stifled the idea, hoping to be as fair-minded about the thing as possible. There was no doubt that Bill Stultz was one of the best pilots and navigators in the business, and his technical skills were more than adequate to the task ahead—if he could just be kept away from the bottle!

Suddenly, on the 17th of June, the weather was right, or about as right as it could be. Stultz was in a half-stupor, and Earhart literally had to drag him to the airplane and get him going. But the *Friendship* did get off this time, rocking and lurching into the wind. Out over the ocean, Stultz seemed to get a grip on himself and was busy at the controls. As the hours ticked by, Earhart knelt down

in the cabin or between the auxiliary gas tanks, anxiously eyeing Stultz and "those little spots of red in the center of his cheeks" which never seemed to disappear as the plane roared onward through the night.

Not quite knowing how to deal with this potentially serious situation, Earhart just waited and hoped for the thing to wear itself out. Her anxieties were not calmed, however, when she found a fresh bottle that Stultz had apparently smuggled aboard before takeoff. What to do with it—slip it through the trap door in the bottom of the fuselage and into the briny deep? No, what if somewhere en route Stultz woke up to his lack of personal fuel and sought out the bottle? Might this not turn him into some wild and irresponsible character? So Amelia decided against this maneuver and left the bottle where it was. As things turned out, Stultz never gave up his cockpit seat and never needed refreshment; his passenger threw the bottle into the Irish Sea at the end of the voyage.

After some doubts near the end of the flight and some fears that fuel would run out before land was sighted, the *Friendship* landed at Burry Port, Wales (not in Southhampton as planned). Almost all of the flight had been under instrument conditions, blind flying, and Stultz had done very well indeed. After a day's rest and re-fueling, the flight was continued to Southhampton, where an enormous welcome was in the making. During this last leg of the trip, Earhart did her first and only stint at the controls. It was, of course, an anticlimax. "The bravest thing I did," Earhart said later, "was to try to drop a bag of oranges and a note on the head of an ocean liner's captain—and missed the whole ship."

The flight across the Atlantic, from Trepassy, Newfoundland, to Burry Port, Wales, took twenty hours and forty minutes. For his role as captain and pilot Bill Stultz received a payment of $20,000 from the flight's backers; Lou Gordon, the mechanic, received $5,000. Amelia Earhart received nothing—nothing, that is, but fame, which was to serve as a springboard to the real career in aviation that was to come. And the adulation was loud and unceasing. Stepping off the plane at Southhampton, Earhart had only the clothes on her back, plus a scarf (later purloined by some members of the press), a comb and a toothbrush. Her intention, she said, was to save space, not to establish trends in international fashion. But so publicized was her lack of wardrobe that weeks later when she arrived in New York by ship with several trunks of luggage, eager customs men were waiting to collect duty on every gift and stitch of clothing in her possession. This hardly mattered, though, in the euphoria following the trip. Earhart was whisked around to visit dignitaries, ambassadors, crowned heads of Europe, all of whom had assumed by now that the achievement was hers and hers alone.

But while the whole world was more than willing to transform Amelia Earhart, teacher of English at Boston's Denison settlement house, into Lady Lindy, conqueror of oceans, Amelia herself was too independent, too honest to believe the ruse. The flight had brought notoriety, but it had not even come close to fulfilling Earhart's own goals in aviation. Moreover, the transatlantic crossing had generated new and probably unexpected problems for Amelia. Publisher George Putnam was not only a shrewd entrepreneur, he also tended to take over the lives of people involved in

his projects. Upon her return from Europe, Amelia began to realize that she had to face not only civic receptions and the writing of a book, but promotional tours, commercial endorsements, fan mail and a variety of related tasks incumbent upon the newly-famous. She would need, Putnam directed, a social and literary secretary, and he would guide the entire enterprise as a sort of manager/agent.

Remarkably, Amelia appears to have accepted these arrangements, at least without expressing any vocal protest, and she lost no time getting down to the task at hand: writing the book she had promised Putnam. She started in April at Putnam's own spacious residence in Rye, New York, and by September, 1928, *20 hrs. 40 min.* was finished. In it she captured not only the events but the feelings she experienced on the famous flight, all in a serviceable and sporty prose. Earhart's writing career began blossoming rapidly. Through Putnam's connections, she became an associate editor of *Cosmopolitan*, agreeing to write eight articles each year on aviation.

Then there were lectures, dozens of them throughout the United States, at universities, colleges, women's clubs and municipal organizations. Amelia Earhart had become, quite simply, the most famous and most sought after woman in America.

And she was making money, lots of it, for the first time in her life. She could write her mother in August of 1928, "Please throw away rags and get things you need on my account at Filene's. I'll instruct them. I can do it now and the pleasure is mine."

In the midst of all this money-making activity, Amelia still found time to consolidate her own experience as a pilot. She became a regular participant in aeronautical competitions like the famous "Powder Puff Derby," a race from Santa Monica to Cleveland, Ohio, which was open only to women and offered a first prize of $2,500. (Will Rogers, Master of Ceremonies for the derby, referred to its entrants as "ladybirds" and "flying flappers," phrases which outraged Earhart, though she and Rogers later became friends.) Amelia did not place first in the 1929 "Powder Puff"; she came in third after Louise Thadden and Gladys O'Donnell. But disappointments of this sort did not deflect her, and she continued setting her own goals. In November of 1929 Amelia excitedly wrote her mother that she believed she had broken the women's speed record with an average time of 184.17 m.p.h. "I did one lap in 197+," she boasted.

Although it is not generally remembered, Amelia's exploits were part of a tradition already, in 1929, almost two decades old. Flying had appealed to women from the very beginning. Only a short time after the Wright Brothers' invention appeared on the scene, women sought to go up in the primitive air machines of the time. The year after Louis Bleriot flew the English Channel (1909), Baroness de la Roche became the first woman ever to receive a pilot's license. An American woman named Harriet Quimby became the first of her sex to receive a license in the United States, and that was in 1911! Quimby was also the first woman to fly across the English Channel, accomplishing that feat in the spring of 1912.

There was, of course, a quality of defiance associated with any woman's desire to fly in the 'teens and twenties. Ruth Nichols defied an edict of her college dean

in order to take flying lessons. Before the decade of the 1920s was over, she had compiled a list of achievements in all phases of aviation that stuffed a record book. Tiny Laura Ingalls enrolled at an eastern flying school, where her male instructors attempted gently to discourage her. It did no good. Ingalls went on to become one of the best stunt pilots of the twenties. During that period she established a woman's record for loops, doing 980 of them consecutively at an air exposition, where she received a dollar a loop.

Pilots like Ruth Nichols and Laura Ingalls were becoming less unusual as the 1920s progressed. A roster of women pilots attaining recognition in that decade would be a long one: Phoebe Omlie, Louise Thadden, Anne Morrow Lindberg, Jacqueline Cochrun, Neta Snook, Mayse Bastie, Bobbie Trout, Edna May Cooper, May Haizlip, Marion Eddy Conrad, Florence Klingensmith, Maude Tait and dozen of others. Even the biggest flights were contemplated by women pilots in the twenties, and by the time Amelia Earhart made her transatlantic crossing with Stultz, a number of other women had already dreamed of doing it. One had even tried. Ruth Elder, with George Haldeman, attempted to fly from Roosevelt Field on Long Island to Europe in the fall of 1927. Unfortunately, they crashed in the Azores, and Ruth Elder gave up aviation for a movie career.

For the most part, these women had not gone into aviation to be pioneers or to prove a point; they were simply overwhelmed and delighted by flight itself. Amelia Earhart "discovered" aviation when her father took her to an airshow in Long Beach, California. Seeing the pilots in the air, the twenty-year-old Amelia became determined to go up and quickly arranged a flight from a tiny field in residential Los Angeles, a mere open space on Wilshire Boulevard surrounded by oil wells. "As soon as we left the ground," she later wrote in *The Fun of It*, "I knew I myself had to fly. Miles away I saw the ocean and the Hollywood hills seemed to peep over the edge of the cockpit, as if they were already friends. 'I think I'd like to learn to fly,' I told the family casually that evening, knowing full well I'd die if I didn't. 'Not a bad idea,' said my father just as casually. 'When do you start?' It would need some investigation I told him, but I'd let him know shortly. Mother seemed equally non-combative."

Earhart got into aviation because it was fun; she stayed in it because it was fun. Of course one couldn't enjoy the fun without being proficient, so she became proficient, and she became supremely professional. She found herself caught up in the excitement of aviation as it existed in the twenties, and stayed with it. But Earhart was never committed to aviation as a lifelong vocation, and was never especially impressed with any need for women to shine in that particular field. Any work, any career, she felt, should be as natural and available to women as to males of the species.

"I've had twenty-eight jobs," she told a group of women in the early thirties. "Experiment! Meet new people. That's better than any college education." Earhart herself had started college, with a view to becoming a doctor. But she gradually abandoned the idea of a medical career as she came to see that the primary attraction, for her, was the scientific—not the humane— aspect of medicine. She was not, she realized, very interested in care-giving. What she *was* interested in was challenge. "You will find the

unexpected everywhere you go in life," she continued to her audience. "By adventuring about, you become accustomed to the unexpected. The unexpected becomes what it really is—the inevitable."

The whole idea of women "adventuring about" *on purpose* was still somewhat shocking even in the thirties, and Amelia Earhart perhaps did not appreciate enough the unusual character which enabled her to do it with a combination of steeliness and breeziness that seems fitting for an aviatrix. She was willing to take the social risks of adventurousness with the same abandon that she brought to the physical risks, and for both she had considerable courage. Although Earhart was by no means a reckless pilot, neither did she ever shrink from the danger which clearly accompanied flying in its early years. Indeed she seems to have sought it out. Perhaps she was partly describing her own motivation when, speaking on the limited opportunities for women in aviation, she criticized *tradition* "which keeps women from trying new things and from putting forth their whole effort once they do venture forth. It also makes men unwilling to recognize women's abilities. Consequently they sometimes feel that they must do foolhardy or silly things just to prove they can."

Very likely, the opportunity to put her feminist views into action was part of the "fun" Earhart found in the world of aviation; and likely too, the challenge of a sceptical masculine world drove her to more and more extreme exploits. There may have been something as well of the Freudian "death wish" at work; she often told her husband that she didn't like the thought of growing old, that she would just as soon go out in a blaze of glory.

But Walter Lippman, in a column written a few days after her presumed death, offered another interpretation. In his view Earhart's "adventuring about" exemplified the finest and the most exciting qualities of the human race.

> The best things of mankind are as useless as Amelia Earhart's adventure. They are the things that are undertaken, not for some definite, measurable result, but because someone, not counting the costs or calculating the consequences, is moved by curiosity, the love of excellence, a point of honor, the compulsion to invent, or inertia which would keep it earth bound forever in its habitual ways. They have in them the free and useless energy with which alone men surpass themselves.
>
> Such energy cannot be planned and managed and made purposeful or weighed by the standards of utility or judged by its social consequences. It is wild and free. But all the heroes, the saints and the seers, the explorers and the creators, partake of it. They do not know what they discover. They can give no account in advance of where they are going, or explain completely where they have been. They are possessed for a time with the extraordinary passion which is unintelligible in ordinary terms.
>
> No preconceived theory fits them. No material purpose actuates them. They do the useless, brave, noble, the divinely foolish and the very wisest things that are done by men. And what they prove to themselves and to others is that man is no mere creature of his habits, no mere automaton in his routine, no mere cog in the collective machine, but that in the dust of which he is made there is also fire, lighted now and then by great winds from the sky.

The picture of Amelia Earhart in her high school yearbook was captioned "the girl in brown who walks alone." This label proved prophetic, as yearbook comments often seem to do. When Earhart finally consented to marry George Putnam, she wore a slightly tatty brown suit and sensible brown shoes—and she seemed as determinedly alone when she walked away from the altar as she had all her life.

Putnam had been resolute in his pursuit of the reluctant Earhart, who declined the first five proposals he made after divorcing his previous wife. Putnam had been her mentor and informal manager since the day she landed, almost literally, in his life after the 1928 flight. On her return from that adventure, Amelia had been lionized beyond the dictates of ordinary sense—treated to ticker tape parades, medals, banquets, surging, shouting crowds, and all the rest. The take-charge personality of Putnam had been something of an anchor against the treacherous currents of celebrity. But marrying him was a different matter.

"I think I may not be able to see marriage except as a cage until I am unfit to work or fly or be active—and of course I wouldn't be desirable then," Amelia wrote to one of her friends. And to her mother, in a short note at the beginning of 1930, Amelia wrote, "I am going west again to pick up my ship. . . . I am not marrying *anybody*." (Another persistent suitor, Sam Chapman, had also been hopeful of getting a "yes" from Earhart, after many years of friendship.) Amelia was determined to pick her own course and was very suspicious of anything—including marriage—which might deflect her from it.

But in the autumn of 1930, Amelia suddenly

reversed herself, and when George Putnam tried again for the sixth time (this time, on a romantic visit to the Burbank Lockheed factory), she accepted. Their "courtship" had been an index of Amelia's attitude toward the whole matter, consisting mainly of brief "dates" at some airport she was flying in or out of, or a few moments together in her *Cosmopolitan* office. And although she was a good writer, her letters to Putnam were even more brief and impersonal than those to her family and friends; for the most part, she just scribbled notes in the margins of his letters to her and mailed them back.

It may have been Earhart's very independence and standoffishness which enthralled Putnam. And for her part, Amelia may have found Putnam's exuberance an attractive reminder of her father; at least this interpretation is suggested by the fact that she finally agreed to marry Putnam shortly after her father died. Edwin Earhart had been an unusual, interesting father, although not entirely a successful one in conventional terms. He was a railroad lawyer whose career was spotty, partly due to his heavy drinking, partly due to his general dreaminess and wanderlust. Mr. Earhart was not one of those fathers who resented having daughters or tried to make up for the lack of male offspring by raising his daughters like sons. But he did encourage Amelia and her sister to ignore propriety and have a good time, in ways which were then thought more appropriate to boys than to "young ladies." The Earhart girls often accompanied their father fishing, carrying their own bamboo rods, cans of worms, and line to string their catch.

Earhart was dearly loved by his daughters, but at

the same time, he proved ill-equipped to provide the kind of stability that children need to feel safe and protected in the world, to make lasting friendships and develop a sense of rootedness. Until Amelia was thirteen, she and her sister enjoyed the advantages of their maternal grandparents' home, a rambling house surrounded by stately maples on a bluff high above the Missouri River. The library there was unusually well-stocked, with all the best children's books as well as the "classics" of adult literature, and Amelia became an avid reader, remaining so all her life. But the gentle life with her grandparents, which balanced the uproarious influence of Edwin Earhart, crumbled away when her grandmother died, and the rest of Amelia's adolescence was rootless and drifting. She attended six different high schools in four years.

But if the conditions of her growing up contributed to Earhart's tendency to be a loner, they also gave her a strong and lasting sense of adventure. Amelia was in some respects very like her father, restless, questing, and playful. One of her college friends recalled Amelia as a high-spirited freshman who quickly found out how to get the key to the roof of the library: "We climbed the endless steps, and up over the roof on hands and knees to the very top of the dome. There we found the freedom of the skies, a world which was secret from our professors." Within a few years, Amelia learned how to take the sky for her own.

When Earhart agreed to marry George Putnam, she was not about to give up the freedom which was so vital to her. Not long before their wedding in 1931, she made this clear in a letter to him:

Dear GP,

There are some things which should be writ before we are married. Things we have talked over before—most of them.

You must know again my reluctance to marry, my feeling that I shatter thereby chances in work which means so much to me. I feel the move just now as foolish as anything I could do. I know there may be compensations, but have no heart to look ahead.

In our life together I shall not hold you to any medieval code of faithfulness to me, nor shall I consider myself bound to you similarly. If we can be honest I think the differences which arise may best be avoided.

Please let us not interfere with each other's work or play, nor let the world see private joys or disagreements. In this connection I may have to keep some place where I can go to be by myself now and then, for I cannot guarantee to endure at all times the confinements of even an attractive cage.

I must exact a cruel promise, and this is that you will let me go in a year if we find no happiness together.

I will try to do my best in every way.

A.E.

Apparently, Earhart lived by the terms expressed in this singularly cool document for the remainder of her life. She did do her "best" as a wife and lived rather tranquilly with Putnam for periods in between flights. Although she was not enthusiastic about matters domestic, she turned out to take some satisfaction in managing her home (at least intermittently). According to Putnam, she could actually cook quite well and had an interesting set of exotic recipes that she collected from her worldwide travels; she always had a very precise count of household supplies, and al-

though she was emphatically not interested in becoming an expert "homemaker," she always insisted on matching the usual accomplishments of the average housewife.

As to the "medieval code of faithfulness" mentioned in her letter to Putnam, whatever liberties she may have taken with it have remained concealed. To be sure, there was gossip about her, linking her romantically to several of the men with whom she worked closely. The wife of one well-known stunt pilot even named Earhart as a corespondent in her divorce suit. But Amelia never seemed bothered by these stories, considering them part of the price one pays for fame. As she wrote her mother, "anyone who has a name in the paper is a target for all sorts of things."

But whatever turns her personal life may have taken, *nothing* distracted Amelia from flying. Between 1928 and 1932, when she made her transatlantic solo, Amelia flew at least 1,000 hours, filling the gaps in her aeronautical education. After her flight with Stultz, the celebrated Amelia had access to the best and latest equipment and plenty of financial backing; her pursuit of the art and technology of aviation during this period was relentless, systematic and wide-ranging. The transatlantic solo, which was an unspoken but assumed goal for Earhart, required mastery of instrument flying—about which she had known little in 1928—and practice, practice, practice. Early in 1932, Earhart casually proposed the flight to her husband as the two of them sat reading the paper, and the most dramatic journey of her career was swiftly in the planning stage.

Although there were no delays in getting started this time, there were plenty of troubles aloft when the event actually took place in May. A few hours after departing from Teterboro airport in New Jersey, her altimeter malfunctioned. Later on she ran into bad icing conditions as she tried to rise above the clouds. Then her tachometer iced over during this ascent. Worse still, the plane began a spin, caused by the heavily iced wings, and she was only barely able to recover before hitting the water. Later on, about two-thirds of the way across, she had a blazing manifold that might have doomed the ship had it completely burned through. But apparently Lady Luck was riding with Lady Lindy in the cockpit, for on May 21, 1932, fourteen hours and fifty-six minutes after leaving Newfoundland, she landed on the farm of James Gallagher in Culmore, Ireland.

"I've come from America," she said to farmhand Dan M'Callion who rushed up to the plane.

Too surprised to know what to say to this strange maid of flight, M'Callion could only utter, "Do ye be tellin' me that now?"

As on her previous flight, Amelia had not given much thought to the media blitz she would encounter on the other side; it was all business as far as she was concerned. Her wardrobe consisted of jodhpurs, a silk shirt, a windbreaker, and a leather flying suit—no dresses, no nightgowns. She had a thermos bottle of soup and a can of tomato juice with a straw for nourishment. "My concern," she wrote, "was simply to fly alone to Europe. Extra clothes and extra food would have been extra weight and extra worry. A pilot whose land plane falls into the Atlantic is not consoled by caviar sandwiches."

In the nearly five years that remained to her, Amelia Earhart planned and executed some long-distance flights that were equal in difficulty to those accomplished by the

best male pilots of her day. In the summer of 1932 she established a speed record for a non-stop transcontinental flight (Los Angeles to Newark) by a woman. The following summer she broke that record, cutting two hours off the flying time. In 1935 she made the first solo flight across the Pacific from Honolulu to California. That same year she was the first to fly solo from Mexico City to New York. These flights were all major undertakings, requiring much advance planning at a time when commercial aviation was still in its infancy and navigational equipment was primitive.

Long distance flights became Amelia's forte. She never developed a taste for loops, stunts, or crowd-pleasing displays. Instead she preferred the purity of aloneness in the sky, the challenge of going further and faster. Although Earhart never developed the pathological hatred of public attention that afflicted Charles Lindberg, still the incessant glare of publicity was wearing for the "girl in brown who walks alone." She took it all with an indifferent good grace, but her long solitary flights were, in part, escapes back into the freedom which had first drawn her to the skies.

On the ground, Amelia lectured—always speaking out firmly on a variety of feminist issues—and wrote. In her three books, she explained clearly, and with a personal, thoughtful tone, her love of flying; she let the reader share with her the exhilaration of exploration and, occasionally, the moments of introspection which were brought about by her adventures. Although Amelia Earhart was very restrained about her private emotions, she opened up completely when it came to flying, for it was through her love of flying that she was finally able to share herself with others.

A poignant passage near the end of her book *Last Flight* captures the breadth of the private world Earhart created for herself with the wonderful tool of flight:

> Not much more than a month ago I was on the other shore of the Pacific, looking westward. This evening I looked eastward over the Pacific. In those fast-moving days which have intervened, the whole width of the world has passed behind us—except this broad ocean. I shall be glad when we have the hazards of its navigations behind us.

There is a joyous, fatalistic daring reflected in this passage, the spirit of an older time. Something of the divine spark of frontier America, with its peril and feeling of rootlessness, was always alive in Earhart.

In 1937, that spirit carried her out over the Pacific, and probably to her death, in an attempt to circle the world. Whatever other considerations may have prompted that final flight —publicity, research, vanity—surely the most important motive was simply to explore another frontier. "I have the feeling there is just about one more good flight left in my system," Earhart told a reporter, standing on the concrete apron while mechanics went over her plane just before the last flight. In obvious terms, the flight was not to be a "good" one. But in another way, perhaps it was. Amelia Earhart simply disappeared, at the height of her fame, never to be diminished by age or illness.

The final puzzle of her disappearance only added to the air of mystery in which Earhart had been shrouded from the beginning. It was clear to everyone that she was not like

"other woman," that she did not conform to the stereotypical role assigned to her sex. Indeed, she didn't seem to fit *any* familiar pattern. There was always an aloof and enigmatic quality about her, an eccentric personal appeal—due in part perhaps to her androgynous quality, her shifting masculine/feminine image. There was the windswept hair, the hint of ruggedness in her features, and yet there was a delicacy about her that seemed to invite the world's affection.

Earhart burst into the public imagination almost as if from nowhere. She seemed to arise magically out of the vast Midwest, like willowy prairie grass appearing unexpectedly in the midst of the city, and to vanish just as suddenly. But in the interim, she created a unique legacy. Amelia Earhart's romance with the sky became one of the better parts of history, a story of courage and purpose and uncommon clarity. While many bright spots of the twenties turned out to be tinsel, Amelia's achievements were real silver, streaks of silver in the blue.

5

MARTHA GRAHAM

After weeks of being drilled in the techniques of modern dance developed by Martha Graham, one young class received its first visit from the celebrated Miss Martha herself, now well into her sixties. Graham watched for a few minutes, then tossed her head and turned away with a single utterance: "Where are the dancers?"

Graham's sweeping, frequently imperial, manner has become almost as legendary as her intensely personal and highly influential approach to dance. But she never expected more of others than she demanded of herself. Martha Graham did nothing halfway—nothing in fact, merely to the full; she seemed to be driven by some burning passion that was always to carry her beyond the threshold of possibility. From the very beginning of her career, Graham worked far into the night and on weekends, driving herself beyond the disciplines of even the most dedicated.

It was this ferocity of spirit which enabled Graham to create an extraordinary career in a field where, by common logic, she shouldn't have been successful at all. Most dancers begin their careers at the age of seven or eight; Martha Graham knew nothing of dance until her late teens, and she began her dance training at the ripe old age of twenty-one. Moreover, in contrast to the tall, willowy body of the typical dancer, Martha Graham's was a compact five feet two inches. Yet Graham not only became a dancer, she became a pre-eminent force in the world of dance, shaping the course of modern dance and creating a permanent legacy of superb choreography.

Graham's career was given a retrospective celebration in 1974, and the power of the great lady—at that time eighty years old—was described by John Gwen:

> The curtain rose at the Mark Hellinger Theatre in New York, and there she stood: Martha Graham—woman, artist, prophet. She stood in shimmering gold and black, and her presence elicited an almost atavistic *fusion* of recognition and love. The audience rose. It cheered. It paid homage to her person, to her art, to her vision, for she embodied dance history—past, present and future.

Incredibly, Graham had stopped dancing only a few years before that night; still more amazing, she has continued to appear with her dance company, maintaining a formidable onstage presence into her nineties.

The sheer drive of Martha Graham seems almost inhuman. And yet the dance forms she has created are human above all, evoking the ancestral past of the race, exploring its psychological depth and physical complexity.

Graham's dances do not merely showcase the talents of a few performers; they speak eloquently of the human condition. "We all inhabit our bodies," Graham once told an audience, "and our most precious garment is our skin, which remains with us from the moment we are born to the moment we are no more. It is a lovely, shining thing."

In a way, Martha Graham's approach to dance seems timeless. It was, however, very much a product of the twenties, a time when intensity and expressiveness ruled the day. New forms were being avidly pursued throughout society in the twenties, and talent like Martha Graham's—innovative, outrageous, authentic—found fertile soil.

"To the universe belongs the dancer" runs an ancient Christian text. "Whoever does not dance does not know what happens." Surely there were a good many people in the audience the evening of April 18, 1926, who did not know what was happening when Martha Graham, part-time teacher at the Eastman School of Music and dancer in the Greenwich Village Follies, staged an independent recital of dance at a rented theater in New York City. The date turned out to be a pivotal one in the history of American dance, although this was not recognized for many years. It clearly marked the beginning of what we now call "modern dance" in this country, and it also launched the independent career of one of America's most remarkable women.

But the concert on that April day had come to pass only through the dynamic force of Martha Graham's will. Among prospective Broadway angels in 1926, there was nary a one who would consider laying out money for a recital devoted to an unknown and probably highly peculiar style of dance, so Graham had to scrounge around for the meager funds needed to put on her program. The largest expense was $1,000 to rent the theater, and this she borrowed from Frances Steloff, who ran the Gotham Book Mart on West Forty-seventh Street. Steloff had never seen Graham dance, but the two had become friends sometime earlier when Graham paid one of many visits to Steloff's shop, a highly individualized establishment that appealed to literary and theatrical folk. Steloff didn't have the slightest idea whether she would ever get her money back; in fact she didn't even have the money in cold cash and had to borrow it at an excessively high rate of interest. But clearly, Martha Graham had worked her spell on this very untypical and farsighted bookseller—as she soon would on a multitude of others.

Graham's company for this concert consisted of the thirty-two-year old Graham herself, and three young dancers—Thelma Biracree, Evelyn Sabin and Betty MacDonald —who had been students of Graham's at the Eastman School, and thus had been relentlessly schooled, drilled and harangued for weeks in Graham's techniques and aesthetic theories. Accompanying the group on the piano was Louis Horst, a composer and musician who in time would become an advisor and confessor not only to Graham but also to a whole generation of young Americans in modern dance. Graham and Horst had met several years earlier when they were both members of Ruth St. Denis's dance company, where the portly, middle-aged Horst, with his air of solidity and permanence, had made himself indispensable. The

impresario for this recital, though, was Graham herself, who had planned the concert down to the smallest detail. She had designed the scenery, even sewn all of the costumes herself —a practice she would continue for years, even after she became one of the leading figures of the dance world. Her ideas on every phase and angle of the dance had been fermenting for several years, and in this ambitious first program she presented them to the public with all the ardor and zeal that she could muster.

Happily, the recital was not a failure. A modest audience turned out, and Frances Steloff got her money back; there was even a small profit. *The New York Times* printed a brief review of the performance, inaccurately maintaining that Martha Graham had offered an evening of interpretive dance to modern music. There *was* modern music, to be sure—Erik Satie and Manuel de Falla, for example—but there were also a suitable number of compositions by Brahms, Schubert and Debussy; more important and innovative than the choice of music was the controlled yet expressive style of movement created by Martha Graham.

The *New York Times* reviewer was not lacking in compliments for Graham, praising her beautiful pictures and stage images, but there was no indication that the evening had been a historic event. A few members of the audience, however, went away believing they had seen something new and remarkable, even if they could not then predict where it would lead. Graham herself may not have realized what a giant step she had made; in later years, she looked back on this and other concerts of the twenties as juvenilia, as "childish awful things." But while there may have been a long way to go, great new things had already happened by that evening on April 18, 1926. Martha Graham had given the world a whole new style—something that was not ballet, not vaudeville, not folk dance, not anything which had quite been seen before.

As all students of history know, and as common sense would suggest, nothing big happens overnight. Graham's first independent recital in 1926 did not simply appear from nowhere. It was part of a stirring movement, almost wholly American in origin, that for some time had been attempting to break down hidebound traditions and conventions in the world of dance. This was not an easy task. In the early years of the twentieth century, classical ballet was the only sort of "serious" dance, and within the ballet world there was very little room for change and development. America, however, had never had a commanding tradition in ballet; in fact, the only good ballet to be seen on the American shore was imported. So it was altogether natural that a new breed of young dancers should look beyond the ballet tradition to something that they could call their own, something novel and native.

Among the first revolutionaries of the dance was Isadora Duncan, who injected a dose of adrenaline into a whole generation of Americans looking for a new style of dance. Early in her career she established an approach to dance based on natural, improvised movements which interpreted music and poetry. Sometimes dancing in loosely draped costumes resembling a Greek tunic, she was the first Western dancer to appear barefoot on stage—quite a scandal at the beginning of the twentieth century. Ever the iconoclast and innovator, breaker of taboos, Duncan believed that

she had been placed on earth to liberate the dance from worn-out formulas and clichés, and to challenge the artificial movements and constricting costumes of classical ballet. Her revolutionary concepts attracted an immediate and sometimes fanatical following, but her career as a dancer was eventually eclipsed by her scandalous private life and torrid love affairs. Nevertheless, she had provided a spark of imagination to an art that had become almost stagnant.

Another prominent precursor of the modern dance, and a rough contemporary of Duncan's, was Ruth St. Denis, born in 1877. Like Duncan, St. Denis loved the exotic and mysterious. An advertising poster for "Egyptian Deities" cigarettes, showing the goddess Isis bare-breasted and seated beneath an imposing stone doorway, made a powerful impression on St. Denis; she was inspired to begin improvising new dance styles, using Egyptian and other exotic flavorings. This adventurous direction proved a complete revitalization for St. Denis. "I knew that my destiny as a dancer had sprung alive," she wrote later. "I would become a rhythmic and impersonal instrument of spiritual revelation rather than a personal actress of comedy or tragedy. I had never before known such an inward shock of rapture."

These Egyptian dances were hardly authentic—they were about as Egyptian as Isadora Duncan's dances were Greek—but they did a great deal to enliven the already fertile mind of Ruth St. Denis. Even more than Duncan, St. Denis was eclectic, willing to borrow from numerous mythological sources and to adapt a wide variety of dance styles. In her *Egypta* (1905), derived in part from her discovery of the vignettes and hymns contained in Wallis Budge's translation of the Egyptian *Book of the Dead*,

St. Denis improvised a goddess who dies, enters the underworld for judgment and, having passed muster, ascends to the Elysian fields. For her performances as the goddess Egypta, St. Denis wrapped a bolt of cloth around her body, assumed a vaguely oriental headdress of jewels and flowers, and wrapped her feet and ankles in ribbons, her version of Egyptian "shoes."

Ruth St. Denis went on to become an extremely influential teacher and choreographer, but her work was still a prelude to the movement called "modern dance," which did not begin to take identifiable form until the late twenties. Even then it was still aborning, and no easy or compact definition was possible. Indeed, there probably could be no single definition of modern dance because it was more a point of view than a body of techniques or a cluster of well-defined philosophies. In the program notes for a concert by Helen Tamiris in 1927, the governing philosophy was stated thus: "There are no general rules. Each work of art creates its own code." Insofar as there was a doctrine of modern dance, it was one of artistic individualism and independence, with each dancer encouraged to develop his or her own choreographic style. Martha Graham expressed this elegantly when she said that each of her works was a "graph of the heart," and thus quite likely to be different from one day to the next.

American modern dancers believed that the dance, to be a valid art form, had to return to the individual expression of the dancer, to elemental human passions and drives. Where earlier forms of the dance had been content to imitate nature, modern dance tried instead to disclose nature, to reveal it. The goal was in part the discovery of

primitive forms of human life and in part the expression, through motion, of states of mind—of the conscious and even the unconscious. Of course, the dancers differed somewhat from one another on which aspects of the human condition the dance should reveal. Doris Humphrey, for example, felt the central concern should be social life, the ideal conditions of humanity. Graham, on the other hand, was more sharply concerned with the hidden recesses of the psyche, as they were revealed through the body. In her focus on this point, Graham raised to high art a cherished fragment of wisdom she had learned from her physician father: that bodily movement can reveal one's inner thoughts and emotions.

Graham located the primary source of the dance in the breath pulse; thus she exaggerated the contractions and expansions of the torso and the flexing of the spine caused by breathing, and she believed that these motions could be employed to reveal man's inner conflicts and passions. To Doris Humphrey, on the other hand, gravity was the source of the dynamic instability of movement; the arc between the balance and imbalance of the body, between fall and recovery, revealed man's conflicts with the world around him. The results of both theories were similar, however, in that they produced something not at all literal. Modern dance was quite different from pantomime. It was meant to be not imitative but suggestive, dramatically provoking the viewer's imagination, rather than leading him to some thoroughly conceptualized point of view.

A great many early spectators of the modern dance found the whole thing to be ungainly, unbeautiful, unfeminine. After Martha Graham's first recital in New York in

1926, one of her friends declared: "It's dreadful, Martha, how long do you expect to keep this up?" And, to be sure, the modern dance of the mid-twenties was as shocking and as unfamiliar as the music of the twelve-tone composers was to its listeners, or as "modern art" had been to the visitors at the great Armory Show a decade earlier. The whole thing was offensive to the untrained eye. It seemed to many, indeed, that modern dance was aggressively trying to overturn everything that was cherished in the ballet. Where the ballet was airborne, attempting to defy gravity (and this foolishly, Graham would say), modern dance hugged the earth; where ballet was pretty and given to fluid motion, modern dance was stark and harshly dramatic.

Another frequent response to modern dance was that it was intellectually austere and bloodless—sexless, perhaps. But how odd. Graham herself believed that her dance was intensely concerned with passion. "Desire is a lovely thing," she said, "and that is where the dance comes from, from desire. And the thing that makes you turn, for a dancer, is the desire to turn first, so that everything comes out in desire; and where does desire reside but between the legs, for most people." Sex was everything for Graham. Yet in another sense it was nothing, it could be nothing until it was melted in the cauldron of the dance, until it was tamed, recast, enslaved. But sex it was. She sought to know and understand nothing else.

For years Graham had no males in her company and even later, when she introduced them, she didn't quite know what to do with them. Her most important creations from first to last—Xochitl, Judith, Eve, Clytemnestra, Joan of Arc, Phaedra, Circe—were powerful and tempestuous

females, women who needed to be seen in the context of the loneliness of their being, or in their bewildering complexity and multifariousness. Graham explored sexuality, not as an unfolding transaction, but as a state of being which infuses all experience. It was not the games between men and women which interested her, but the way in which sex, desire, shapes the world.

The history of modern dance and the life of Martha Graham are almost inseparable—not only because her work was at the center of the development of modern dance, but also because dance *was* her life. Yet she came to dance by a curious and delayed route.

There was little in Martha Graham's early life that would have pointed in the direction of a career in dance. She was not born with little dancing feet, and she grew up in an environment where dance in any of its forms was virtually unknown. Graham was born in the dark and brooding hills of western Pennsylvania in the town of Allegheny, a town that has subsequently been swallowed up in present-day Pittsburg. With the coal mines and the steel mills nearby, the area was one of persistent grime and grayness, of resistance to beauty in all its forms—indeed, H. L. Mencken, traveling by train through western Pennsylvania, insisted that the people there had a positive libido for the ugly, that they built for themselves houses singularly insulting to the eye, that a pall of gloom had fallen over these hills and valleys that had no connection with the poverty of the land or the environs. It was seemingly a place in which people had allowed themselves to be suffocated in spirit out of all proportion to any ascertainable cause.

Allegheny was certainly gray and depressing, but even more surely, it was no center of cosmopolitan delights or advanced thinking, and Martha remembered the place as stifling and restrictive. Her family life, however, was reasonably pleasant. George Graham, a physician who treated the mentally ill, was quite a bit older than his three daughters, and he maintained a severe aloofness, but in many respects he seems to have been a rather liberal and thoughtful father. Martha became an omnivorous reader at an early age, and her father encouraged her and permitted her access to his extensive library. Unlike many fathers of the day, even in more enlightened parts of the country, Dr. Graham had hopes of securing a college education for each of his daughters.

When Martha was fourteen, the Graham family moved from Pennsylvania to southern California, and this transition from the grim hills of the coal country to the riotous color of California undoubtedly had much to do with changing the direction of Martha's life. Years later, in an interview with *Dance Magazine*, Graham spoke of this new climate in almost revolutionary terms:

> My people were strict religionists who felt that dancing was a sin. They frowned on all worldly pleasures. . . . My upbringing led me to fear it myself. But luckily we moved to Santa Barbara, California. . . . No child can develop as a real Puritan in a semi-tropical climate. California swung me in the direction of paganism, though years were to pass before I was fully emancipated.

This description is something of an oversimplification, for although Graham may have wriggled out from under the heavy yoke of Puritanism, she cannot be said to have simply dismissed the cold and austere Presbyterianism of her girlhood. Rather, it would seem that she ploughed it under, so to speak, and let it grow anew in other and more powerful forms. In spite of all her protests to the contrary, Graham's mature work as a dancer remained infused with tautness and restraint, and she could be as harsh in the professional requirements she made of herself and her followers as some fire and brimstone Calvinist. It is certainly true, though, that when her family moved to California in 1908, a whole new feeling of freedom overtook Martha. She was immediately and joyfully grateful for the open spaces, the nearness of the ocean, the lush tropical plants, the exotic cultures—Black, Mexican, Chinese—found in the area. This new-found paradise, Graham came to believe, was responsible for kindling her expressive powers and her sense of motion.

Physical activity and expression were important to her from an early age, and before she knew about dance, sports seemed the only outlet for this energy. Martha was strongly athletic at Santa Barbara High School and, in bloomers and middy blouse, played basketball with a fierce intensity. Then Dr. Graham, who had kept his medical practice in Pennsylvania, came out to the West Coast on one of his periodic visits and, while there, decided to give his eldest daughter a special treat. They agreed on attending a dance concert given by the company of Ruth St. Denis. What Graham saw on that warm summer night in 1911 was *Egypta*, the ballet inspired by a cigarette poster in Buffalo,

New York. According to the program notes, it began this way:

> Egypta, wearing a transparent, ribbed tunic and black wig, descends the stairway. . . . She carries a flower-chain in each arm and walks in undulating rhythms to the water's edge. . . . Bending low, her chest almost grazing the water, Egypta begins her invocation to the Nile. She lifts her arms in sinuous ripples toward the heavens, suggesting the rising of the waters. As her arms spiral, she gradually rises from her knee to stand with her arms outstretched, palms upturned. She reascends the stairway and enters the temple gates.

The impact of this performance on young Martha Graham was apparently magical: she gave up the basketball team and took up dramatics.

Shortly after graduating from Santa Barbara High in 1913, she persuaded her parents to let her attend the Cumnock School in Los Angeles, a private institution that offered both high school and junior college subjects, but was specifically oriented toward self-expression in theater, art, dance and music. Graham stayed for three years at the Cumnock School, receiving a certificate, but she still had no clear idea of her educational objectives. Nevertheless, she timidly entered the 1916 summer classes at the Denishawn School to sit at the very feet of "Egypta," Ruth St. Denis.

Judged by all the conventional standards of the dance, Graham was a very unlikely prospect. Traditional training in ballet usually begins very early, and pupils who come in as adults are not considered malleable. Even the broader concept of the dance being taught and advocated at Denishawn and exhibited around the country by Miss

Ruth herself did not hold out any promise of a professional career for someone Graham's age. Ruth St. Denis was not enthusiastic about Martha, and later recalled that she was "exceedingly shy and quiet, with the same fascinating, homely face that she has today. Most of the time in my class she sat very still and listened." Perhaps, as this rather catty remark suggests, St. Denis actually saw in Graham a potential rival. In any event, it was Ted Shawn, St. Denis's husband and partner, who accepted Graham as his personal charge and agreed to instruct her himself. Almost immediately, the "unteachable" Martha Graham proved herself something of a minor miracle. By the end of her first summer at Denishawn, Graham had become one of the most adaptable and promising dancers in the school. Shawn was delighted, and even St. Denis finally began using Graham as a demonstrator in her own classes.

Early in 1919, Ted Shawn and Ruth St. Denis forged one of their many "agreements to disagree," and the Denishawn School was dismantled. Ted opened his own studio in Los Angeles, assisted by a pianist and a single dancer—Martha Graham. It was while Graham was working as Shawn's assistant that she got her first big chance to perform a memorable role. The vehicle was a "native American ballet," *Xochitl*. Shawn had actually conceived *Xochitl* as vaudeville, a "dance spectacle" based on the Toltec legend of an aging emperor's lust for a nubile dancing girl. A musical score had been commissioned from Homer Grunn, an expert on southwestern Indian music; sets and costumes were designed by Francisco Cornejo, a recognized authority in the field of Aztec-Toltec art. Rather unexpectedly, *Xochitl*, when taken on tour, was a triumph for Shawn and his new dance company. Critics called the work "utterly original," and audiences loved it—in large part because of Graham's performance.

The title role in *Xochitl* seemed tailor-made for Graham. As the show opens, Xochitl and some other dancing girls are seated before a highly stylized Mexican setting, complete with a ziggurat and exotic plants. Xochitl's father arrives, staggering and obviously drunk: he has discovered how to make *pulque*, an intoxicant, out of the local plants, and the group eventually decides to take a sample of the drink to the Emperor. The peasants pass the bowl of *pulque* to the Emperor, and he begins to sip it. Quickly warmed and aroused by the drink, the Emperor motions to Xochitl to dance for him. (Here Graham began her first solo, a series of meltingly graceful poses.) However, as the Emperor becomes progressively inebriated from the strong drink, his lust for the diminutive dancer is aroused, and the tone of the story—and of the dance—changes rapidly. The Emperor, having persuaded some of the girls to lure Xochitl's father away, begins his own frenzied dance, building to an assault on the young dancer.

The story ends happily, as the Emperor eventually marries Xochitl, but the powerful rape scene gave Graham a chance to display her Dionysian talents and dazzling theatricality to the utmost. Ted Shawn, who played the Emperor, later recalled that when the show was being rehearsed and performed, Graham attacked him with such intensity in the rape scene that his lips were left bruised and bleeding, in spite of all his efforts to ward off her blows. Graham had so completely submerged herself in this violent role that she had, in effect, *become* the ferocious Xochitl.

Critics may have praised the originality of *Xochitl*, but there were also highly vocal detractors. Works such as this one inspired bitter opposition in America's heartland, notably from fundamentalist preachers, who accused this "modern dance" of a variety of sins. One of the most popular diatribes against the new style of dance was *The Modern Dance: A Historical and Analytical Treatment of the Subject*, by Mordicai Ham, a Texas preacher of diminished intelligence and pseudoscientific methodology. Dancing of this kind, Ham claimed, led to broken homes, illegitimate offspring, war and disease. Arguments were adduced from "psychologists," physicians and social workers, and Ham's text was further embellished by lurid subtitles—"Men Must Fondle Girls' Feet" and "Undergarments Worn for Public View." To clinch his argument, the author included in his work photographs of his two baby daughters, with the caption "Two Reasons Why I Fight The Dance." Whether the Reverend Ham ever attended a performance of *Xochitl* is doubtful, but his views certainly reflected fears common in "middle America" as the 1920s began.

Xochitl was just the beginning of Graham's association with the Denishawn Company, which continued for the next three years. Ultimately, though, a break even with Shawn's troupe was inevitable for the strong-willed Graham, and it came in 1923 when, on one of her many tours with Shawn, she was seen by John Murray Anderson. Anderson offered her a leading role in the Greenwich Village Follies, at much more lucrative wages. To be sure it was commercial show business, and not the kind of thing that Graham eventually wanted to do, but her motives are familiar to all those who remain apprentices too long. Graham was hell-bent for independence, calculating that artistic integrity would follow at the right moment.

On Graham's final tour with Ted Shawn, she was also noticed by someone else who was to further her route to independence. This was the young Russian-born theater director Rouben Mamoulian, who had recently made a great success staging plays and operas in London and Paris. (He was also to become a prominent Hollywood movie director in the 1930s.) Mamoulian came to the United States at the invitation of George Eastman, who was opening a school of music at Rochester, New York, and needed someone to run the section on dramatic arts. This section was eventually expanded to include instruction in the dance, and Mamoulian, who had been very impressed with Graham, thought that she would work in supremely well with the plans he had for the development of a dance program at Eastman. So in the fall of 1924, Graham took up teaching duties there.

Martha Graham, like Ruth St. Denis, never relished the art of teaching. But her new teaching role had the powerful side effect of giving her the freedom she needed to develop her own concepts of dance and the opportunity to assemble a company of dancers proficient in her methods. Her association with Eastman brought together all the elements that would make possible her momentous first recital. It was while at Eastman that Graham renewed a long friendship with the musician Louis Horst, who, after ten years as its musical director, had also dropped out of Denishawn. Horst had been abroad in Vienna, and for a time had hoped to make his own independent way as a composer, but after

an extended correspondence with Graham, he was persuaded to return to the United States and help her struggling ensemble get on its feet.

Horst, an enthusiastic admirer of Graham's, was convinced of her genius from their earlier associations; indeed, he had been one of the strongest supporters of Graham's desire to bolt from Ted Shawn's troupe. But there was more between the two than just professional admiration. Graham and Horst had emotional ties which were only partly impeded by the fact that Horst was married. The dancer and the musician seemed perfectly suited to one another; Horst was a big, overstuffed teddy bear of a man, jovial and sentimental, loving the German comforts of beer, heavy foods and *Gemütlichkeit*—precisely the right characteristics to counterbalance the frenetic and high-strung Graham. Furthermore, Horst had an extensive knowledge of art, music and world culture generally, areas in which Graham considered herself to be deficient. So their relationship was a sympathetic one in many ways.

Horst was one of the few people who was ever really close to Graham. She did marry in the late thirties—a brilliant young dancer named Eric Hawkins—but the partnership was brief. By then Graham was adulated by students and by the public, her very eminence in the world of dance placing her on a lonely and windswept plane. In the forties, even her ties with Horst were broken when the two quarreled irreparably. After that, Graham drifted ever more resolutely toward self-imposed isolation, cultivating as both teacher and public person an aloof, austere manner which frequently kept others at bay. The ice-queen image is probably not the real Martha Graham, but she perfected it to such an extent that she may also have come to believe in it herself.

In truth, there seems to have been no room in Martha Graham's life for anything which detracted from her intense devotion to the dance. Whether or not this was what she wished is difficult to tell; there was a kind of fatedness about her involvement with dance which she herself sensed. "I don't think I chose dance," she told an interviewer in 1982. "Dance chose me. And it was time for someone to emerge in that way I did. Something was haunting me. I call it 'the ancestral footstep.' I had to go on and on and on." Perhaps Graham found herself confined by the demands of an art that needed change, demands which drove everything else out of her life. Yet she certainly does not appear to have felt deprived, nor does she resent the arduous life she has led in the service of dance. As she told the audience which gathered to honor her in 1974, "It is not grim to be a dancer. Dancing is not a denial, it is an affirmation."

Just what is affirmed and made real in the dance is not expressible in words, Graham feels. When a young dance-enthusiast rushed up to her after seeing a performance of one of her new works and asked breathlessly to know what the marvelous dance meant, Graham replied simply, "Darling, if I had known what it meant I wouldn't have danced it." Dancing was never for Martha Graham the expression of thought, but rather "a revelation of the interior landscape of man," a making-visible of things which never really *can* be thought. It was to achieve this level of truth in dance that Martha Graham became a revolutionary.

"I had no idea of being an innovator or a non-conformist," she says of her early career. "I simply knew things were not the way I wanted them to be. . . . I felt those hidden things in life that we don't show anybody were essential for me to reveal."

The struggle she waged to establish her version of the dance was formidable, and she herself concedes that she was "vain and arrogant" in pushing forward her ideas. But creative struggle is part—perhaps the most important part—of living for Martha Graham. As she said in an interview in 1983:

> All of life is a combat. First with yourself, then later with outside things. I have great respect for the dragon. He is the epitome of good and bad, and everyone's life—with some exceptions, I suppose—is made up of good and bad. The dragon has definitely ominous, yet delightful, meaning for me. He is a stimulant.

PART THREE

Graphs of the Heart

6

EDNA ST. VINCENT MILLAY

In the summer of 1948, Edmund Wilson saw Edna St. Vincent Millay again, almost thirty years after the end of their uneasy courtship. "I felt, just as I had when she was young," he wrote, "that I was being sucked into her narrow and noble world, where all that mattered was herself and her poetry, and I felt the need to break away from it."

Wilson was not the only one of Millay's friends and lovers to retreat from the intensity with which she lived—an intensity perfectly described in one of the simple and stunningly direct poems with which Millay captured the public imagination in the twenties:

> My candle burns at both ends;
> It will not last the night;
> But ah, my foes, and oh, my friends—
> It gives a lovely light!

This small poem became almost a slogan for the awakening postwar generation. Millay had, in expressing something essential about herself, at the same time created a potent symbol for the age in which she lived.

Millay never set out to be a symbol, however; she set out to be a serious poet, and her efforts to achieve this continued, with a determination both fierce and poignant, to the end of her life. She wrote copiously—poems and plays, fiction, translations—through more than four decades of social turmoil and personal difficulty. Constantly along the way she tried, and failed, to still her nervousness, to find a haven from her own passions.

In her fifty-eighth year, when the candle finally burned through, Millay was found dead in a tableau which seemed to summarize her life: she lay at the foot of the stairs of her farmhouse, page proofs of Rolfe Humphries's translation of Catullus scattered about, an unfinished glass of wine at her side. A fragment of a final poem was scribbled in her notebook:

> I will control myself or go inside
> I will not flaw perfection with my grief
> Handsome this day; no matter who has died.

"She came running around the corner of Macdougal Street in Greenwich Village, flushed and laughing like a nymph, with her shoulder-length hair swinging." That was how Phyllis Duganne remembered Edna St. Vincent Millay at the beginning of the twenties.

No one who knew Edna Millay—as the astonishing nineteen-year-old poet of "Renascence" or as the prematurely aged recluse of Steepletop farm—ever failed to mention how she *looked:* her beautiful red hair, her green, shining eyes and Irish complexion. Millay's looks tugged powerfully at the memories and imaginations of the men and women who found their way into her world. But although her attractiveness, especially her sexual appeal, was compelling, it was the kind that escapes easy categorization. "She was one of those women," Edmund Wilson remembered, "whose features are not perfect and who in their moments of dimness may not even seem pretty but who, excited by the blood or spirit, become almost supernaturally beautiful."

When the twenties began, Edna's personal magnetism and her strong poems had already won a small, delicate reputation among her fellow urban bohemians in Greenwich Village. She had published a number of serious poems in the newly influential magazine *Poetry,* as well as in *The Dial* and *Ainslee's Magazine;* a small collection of her early poems had been issued in 1917 under the title *Renascence and Other Poems*. But even in the best of times we are not a people who take our poets to heart, and the name Edna St. Vincent Millay would scarcely have sparked a gleam of recognition outside her tiny circle of intellectuals, actors and other poets.

All of this was to change with suddenness, however, in the fall of 1920, when Millay issued a volume of light verse called *A Few Figs From Thistles*. It was nothing more than a pamphlet, really, a little chapbook in a green cover, published by a sympathetic Greenwich Village bookshop owner. But somehow—and no one can explain exactly how, for the book enjoyed none of the efforts of modern promotion, or indeed, much of any promotion at all—*A Few Figs From Thistles* made a national celebrity of Edna St. Vincent Millay.

This inexplicable alchemy of communication was as much a surprise to Millay as it was to everyone else. She had been desperately hoping that her next book of serious poems, to be entitled *Second April*, would make some money, but the promises of publication never materialized; in frustration, she extracted some of her lighter poems from the larger collection, and these became the substance of *Figs*. The fresh, flippant quality of the poems surprised and delighted readers:

> And if I loved you Wednesday,
> Well what is that to you?
> I do not love you Thursday—
> So much is true.

To a war-weary America, looking for liberation from stale moral values, Millay's voice was that of a new generation. Her viewpoint was one that youth could understand, and the words of her simple poems spread, like the 1918 influenza epidemic, to every part of the country.

Women, especially, were gripped by the new sense of power and freedom expressed in Millay's poems. There was an invigorating insouciance in lines such as these:

> Oh, think not I am faithful to a vow!
> Faithless am I save to love's self alone.
> Were you not lovely I would leave you now:
> After the feet of beauty fly my own.

Her poems captured the first glimmerings of a new sexual freedom for women, an escape from the sticky bonds of "romance" to a new control over their own emotional lives. *A Few Figs From Thistles* became ubiquitous on the campuses of women's colleges, its green cover a symbol of feminist feeling that went far deeper than the desire for political equality which had just been somewhat appeased by the passage of the nineteenth amendment. Millay's poems spoke of a change in the substratum of the social fabric, a psychological transformation more sweeping—and devastating—than most people yet realized.

It was the convergence of two strong gifts—one for poetry, the other for life—in Edna St. Vincent Millay which made her the perfect focus for the fears and fantasies of a nation in transition. Young women were changing, in ways of which they were only just becoming aware; Millay's poetry gave clear voice to these changes, because she herself was living them. Her poems grew out of the fierce independence, the unrepentant sexuality, and the consuming awareness of the moment which made Millay the quintessence of the "new" American woman.

It was easy, then, for a popular, simplistic view of Millay to take shape. She *was*, after all, unattached and irresponsible—an actress, a free-love poetess, a dropout from all the conventional social values, a dweller in the ateliers of debauchery which lined the streets of Greenwich Village. To other young women who scented the new freedom and longed to enjoy it, Millay was a heroine; to many of their parents, however, she was a harbinger of the decline of Western civilization.

But history is always too complex to produce a

wholly representative type, and human nature is too complicated for any individual to be the unalloyed archetype of an age. It was true that Edna Millay lived in Greenwich Village, and that she attracted the attention of a great many males—more, in fact, than she knew what to do with. But she was also a disciplined poet, with an almost fanatical dedication to her art. Millay was by no means an example of "flaming youth"; in 1920 she was already twenty-eight, a graduate of Vassar, an experienced actress and playwright, and a published writer.

Greenwich Village was, in fact, a brief interlude in Millay's life, although it was central to her experience and to her reputation. The Village was the vortex of creative happenings after the war, and Millay went there because of its proximity to other poets and intellectuals; cheap rent and artistic stimulation were more important attractions of the Village than its supposed immorality. But she never fitted perfectly into the Village or into any other milieu. She was deeply a creature of solitude, whose involvements with other people seemed always to be "messes," and for whom the dispassionate world of the sea, the garden, and the woods were to prove the only lasting comfort.

Millay remained throughout her life a kind of spartan New Englander, with something of a rocky and salty air that could be easily misconstrued by those unfamiliar with this cold and infertile land where crops grow only with difficulty and common sense dictates that the farms should be turned back to timber. Her life began on the rocky seacoast of Maine, where the snow comes early and the wind whips in from the ferocious Atlantic. In fact, her curious middle name was a reminder of the dangers of the

sea. Her mother's brother, a sailor, had been injured in a storm, and was cared for at St. Vincent's Hospital; the name St. Vincent was chosen, in gratitude, for the baby her mother firmly expected to be a boy. When a girl appeared instead, the first name Edna was added on, but "Vincent" remained her familiar name, used by family and close friends, throughout Millay's life. Perhaps this was an echo of Providence, for St. Vincent was the patron saint not only of the sick, but also of drunkards, and Edna was to have long experience of both illness and alcohol.

Millay's early life was not idyllic, but neither was it tragic. Although her father was an habitual gambler, wayward and elusive, who brought difficulty to the family, her mother was by all accounts a remarkable woman who gave Edna and her two sisters, Norma and Kathleen, a secure and unusually creative life. Cora Millay took the then-unusual step of divorcing her husband when Edna was eight years old, and Edna had little to say of her father in later years, although she seems to have loved him dearly. The fears and feelings of abandonment which run through Millay's poetry may have been in part a response to the loss of her father, but on the brighter side, the directness and courage which also filled her poems had a rich source in her mother's unusual character.

Edmund Wilson sketched an appreciation of Cora Millay when he met her in the early twenties, gathered with her daughters for a summer on Cape Cod.

> She sat up straight and smoked cigarettes and quizzically followed the conversation. She looked not unlike a New England school teacher, yet there was something almost raffish about her. She had

> anticipated the Bohemianism of her daughters, and she sometimes made remarks that were startling from the lips of an old lady. But there was nothing sordid about her; you felt even more than with Edna that she had passed beyond good and evil, beyond the power of hardship to worry her, and that she had attained there a certain gaiety.

Wilson found himself completely overpowered by these spirited and nonconformist females, whose world was as strongly fortified as it was jaunty. At its center was Cora, who had not only raised three children alone, but had provided them with a homelife extraordinary by the standards of that time, or even of our own, a life filled with books and music, and with affection. When Edna began, at the age of eleven or twelve, to keep a notebook of her poems (rather grandly titled "The Poetical Works of E. St. Vincent Millay"), she wrote on the first page: "To my mother, whose interest and understanding have been the life of many of these works, and inspiration of many more, I lovingly dedicate this volume."

Cora's personality was certainly an influence on her daughter's development as a poet; so too was the town of Camden, where Edna grew up, in an old house on a tree-lined street. Camden offered both the settled civility of New England smalltown life and a rich exposure to the world of nature. Built around a snug harbor on Penobscot Bay, Camden was set in the midst of three long mountains that rose abruptly from the bay in a series of cliffs. Except for the beaches, where Edna joined other children in collecting shells and digging for clams and mussels, the sleepy town was carved out of the rock; the surrounding terrain was covered with tall pines that invited hikers, wildflower-seekers, and

any who hoped to commune with the darker spirits of nature. Edna herself loved these tall pines, but perhaps even more, she loved sitting out on one of the rocks alone by the sea, where she could listen to the endless pounding of the surf against the rocks; where in winter and on gray days the fog bells called out their warning to sailors. There were grim hulks of shipwrecked vessels to remind one of the tragic inevitability of the sea, the powerlessness of man to struggle against the forces of nature. At the age of ten Edna herself almost drowned in the sea, an experience that clearly influenced her first important poem, "Renascence," and doubtless much of her later poetry as well.

"Renascence" was written when Millay was nineteen, four years after her first published poem had appeared in *St. Nicholas*, a prestigious children's magazine. The literary standards of *St. Nicholas* were high, and Millay's numerous contributions established her as something of a poetic prodigy. Her adolescence was, however, if not typical, certainly normal enough: she read omnivorously, was a bit of a tomboy, acted in school plays, and had at least one ill-fated teenage romance. To the casual viewer, the intense gift she possessed was more suggested than revealed as Millay came of age in Camden.

The long, dark poem "Renascence" made indisputable the remarkable talent which was biding its time as Millay, with no money for college, remained at home to care for her sisters. Even for a poet of mature years a work of two hundred and fourteen lines, in tetrameter couplets, is a serious undertaking; for a girl of nineteen, it was astonishing. The poem possessed a youthful freshness and vitality, and yet at the same time its cosmic sweep and its ceaseless philosophical probing seemed to grow out of the solid ground of nineteenth-century transcendentalism. This impression of an innocent voice speaking the knowledge of old verities was described by Louis Untermeyer, who said of the poem, "It is as if a child playing . . . had, in the midst of prattling, uttered some shining and terrible truth." The terrible truth is the immensity and dangerousness of the universe, the fragility of human life against the hand of fate.

"Renascence" was to become the most famous and durable of Millay's poems, but its ritual glorification in innumerable high-school textbooks may have done it more harm than good. The fact that Millay wrote it as an adolescent does not necessarily make the poem meaningful to other adolescents; in fact, most of us who had to read "Renascence" in high school took the simple surface for the poem, and never looked further. While it is true that "Renascence" is an extremely simple poem, of the sort that can be appreciated even by those uncomfortable with the compactness and complex imagery of the poetic art, it is also true that, seen more deeply, the poem is a sophisticated, powerfully affecting work of feminine feeling, and of creative sensibility.

It is, too, an intimate study of Millay's life at nineteen, hemmed in by the mountains, by the sea of Penobscot Bay, by the tall dark firs. In the poem, the sky seems to offer the only way out, but the young protagonist reaches up and finds that here, too, there is no escape. The sky is so low that she can touch it; she must now be weighted down by the whole burden of eternity, as if all human guilt, all human suffering were hers. Still later she sinks into the ground, into a grave, images suggesting the ultimate imprisonment of her surroundings. Soon, however, this fear of death is washed away by the rain, a storm—perhaps hinting

at sexual love—which sets her free to enjoy all the beauties she has longed for in the world, and reminds her of the vast possibilities of eternity, the promise given to the spirit that refuses to die.

"Renascence" states a theme that would continue to be central to Millay's work. She is alone, afraid that the world will crush her, that she might die before having the opportunity to come back to life. It is a struggle never completely won; again and again she must assert her identity and freshness of soul to stay alive, a point made with simple effectiveness in the final lines:

> The world stands out on either side
> No wider than the heart is wide;
> Above the world is stretched the sky,—
> No higher than the soul is high.
> The heart can push the sea and land
> Farther away on either hand;
> The soul can split the sky in two,
> And let the face of God shine through.
> But East and West will pinch the heart
> That cannot keep them pushed apart;
> And he whose soul is flat—the sky
> Will cave in on him by and by.

The twin poles of claustrophobia and freedom, of flatness and beauty, of death and life—so movingly presented in "Renascence"—were to provide the energy and dynamism of all Millay's poetry. These were the motifs not only of her work but of her being, and the tortured struggle played out in the field between these poles was to shape the rest of her life.

Miss Caroline B. Dow, head of the National Training school of the YWCA, was a genteel southern lady who yearly took refuge from her administrative duties and enjoyed the summer at Camden. There she heard Edna Millay read some of her poems. She was moved especially by "Renascence," perhaps hearing in it the poet's need for a wider world, a higher sky. Miss Dow offered to send Millay to college, and at twenty-one the young poet began a rewarding but often tumultuous stay at one of the nation's most exclusive women's colleges.

"Renascence" had already been published in an anthology entitled *The Lyric Year*, and its appearance had occasioned a small storm of controversy which brought Millay to the attention of her fellow poets. The editors of the volume had offered a prize for the best poem of the year, and the chief editor, Ferdinand Earle, had believed that "Renascence" should win. His colleagues, however, were not keen on giving the prize to a virtual unknown; finally the poem received only an honorable mention. This injustice sparked an uproar in poetry circles, and E. St. Vincent Millay began to receive correspondence from other poets, some of whom—including Witter Bynner and Arthur Davison Ficke—were to become lifelong friends.

Older in years than the typical freshman, and far more mature intellectually than most, Millay found Vassar frustrating as well as rewarding. Millay regarded herself as an adult and a completely independent individual; since she had not been supervised at home for years, she saw no need for the college to monitor her behavior. "I hate this pink-and-gray college," she wrote to Arthur Ficke. "If there had been a college in *Alice in Wonderland* it would be this

college . . . We can go into the candy kitchen and take what we like and pay or not and nobody is there to know. But a man is forbidden as if he were an apple."

Millay had something of her own revenge on the untrusting monitors, however, and took copious enjoyment in flaunting the rules and regulations. She refused to stop smoking (like her mother and sisters, she had smoked long before most women dreamed of taking up the practice), even though it meant sneaking off campus and cutting classes. Her excuses were offered in an audacious and cavalier manner, as when she explained that she had been absent from chapel because "It was raining and I was afraid the red on the pew would fade on my new dress."

In truth, though, Millay did not really hate Vassar, and she flourished mightily there, studying seriously not only English literature, but French, Latin, Greek, Spanish, German and Italian. She formed deep and lasting friendships, wrote poems for the *Vassar Miscellany*, intensified her interest in the theater. By the time she left Vassar, Millay was an experienced and educated young woman, with a strong sense of identity and purpose. She arrived in New York ready for life—although not, perhaps, for the one she was to have.

Edna Millay had been too strong, too aloof, too unusual to attract the local boys in Camden, but these same qualities drew fascinated attention from the male population of Greenwich Village almost instantly. One of her first romantic liaisons was with Floyd Dell, then coeditor with Max Eastman of the left-leaning *The Masses*. From the beginning, Millay's personal and professional lives were closely intertwined, and it was Dell who brought her to the attention of George Cram (Jig) Cook and his wife Susan Glaspell, who were running a small playhouse at 139 Macdougal Street—the Provincetown Players, it was called, because it had been established in 1915 on a wharf in Provincetown, Massachusetts. The group was originally a subscription theater formed with the aim of "giving American playwrights a chance to work out their ideas in freedom," and in time it proved to be an excellent springboard for writers as different as Millay, Eugene O'Neill, Maxwell Anderson and e.e. cummings. Millay's career with the Provincetown Players was launched when she took an ingenue part in Floyd Dell's *The Angel Intrudes*; later, she made several very significant contributions of her own to the company's repertoire.

It was her gift for the dramatic, in part, which drew a steady stream of suitors to Millay—among them, Edmund Wilson, who was to become one of America's great men of letters. He had read and admired her poems in the *Vassar Miscellany* before the two met at a Greenwich Village party where Millay had been invited to read some of her verse. Wilson was totally charmed by her recitation, and later tried to analyze Millay's magnetism, which, he said, affected people of both sexes, small children—even birds. Millay was a diminutive woman, barely five feet tall, but "her figure was full, though she did not appear plump. She had a lovely and very long throat that gave her the look of a muse." A vibrant intensity seemed to infuse her voice, her body, her movements. "She pronounced every syllable distinctly," he recalled, and "gave every sound its value."

There was something in Millay's character, how-

ever, "as different as possible from the legend of her Greenwich Village reputation, something austere and grim." Although she could be amusing in company, she was never what might be called a social person. She did not gossip, nor did she enjoy dissecting personalities. And her relations with her admirers, Wilson noted, were curiously impartial; while she reacted to the personalities of the men she knew or to other traits such as voice, she gave the impression that personal qualities did not matter to her much except as subjects for poems. She was, said Wilson, "sometimes rather a strain, because nothing could be casual for her; I do not think I ever saw her relaxed, even when she was tired or ill. . . . She was like the most condensed literature or music, the demands of which one cannot meet protractedly, or like a serious nervous case."

In spite of her poetic intensity, in spite of her harsh detachment and often unpredictable states of mind, Wilson found Millay fascinating and proposed to her in the summer of 1920 when he visited the Millay family on Cape Cod. Her answer was something of a mystery, apparently. "She did not reject my proposal, but said that she would think about it. I am not sure that she actually said, 'that might be the solution,' but it haunts me that she conveyed the idea. In any case, it was plain to me that proposals of marriage were not the source of great excitement."

Although marriage to Wilson was not the "solution" Millay was looking for, like all of her lovers he became an important influence on her career. Wilson was then an assistant editor of *Vanity Fair*, as was John Peale Bishop, who also fell in love with Millay. Both recommended her work to the elegant, silver-haired editor of *Vanity Fair*, Frank Crowninshield, who had already shown an uncommon knack for discovering new talent; it was he who brought Dorothy Parker to the attention of the public on the pages of *Vogue*, another of his magazines. *Vanity Fair* became an important vehicle for much of Millay's literary output in the early twenties. She published some of her most important lyric poetry there under her own name, along with commercial stories and novelettes which she insisted appear under the pseudonym "Nancy Boyd."

"Have you noticed," Millay wrote in a letter in the fall of 1920, "how *Vanity Fair* is featuring me of late? They just can't seem to go to print without me. And the *New Republic* is writing to me in longhand begging for a crumb of verse. Ain't it wonderful?" It was indeed—but it was also problematic. Success did not exactly spoil Edna St. Vincent Millay, but it did create conflicts she was not entirely ready or able to deal with. Between the rising demand for her work and the seemingly endless stream of male admirers, Millay was constantly under strain, and like the proverbial "impractical poet," she was careless about her health, her personal affairs, the world of the mundane generally; she drank too much, ate irregularly, and generally lived up to her own poetry. Her candle, burning at both ends, gave a brilliant—but flickering—light.

The desperate activity with which Millay filled her life during these years was at least in part an attempt to assuage a deep sadness. A poem she recited one day in 1920 to Edmund Wilson, as they rode the Fifth Avenue bus, revealed with bitter poignancy the loss not merely of a lover, but of love itself:

Here is a wound that will not heal, I know,
Being wrought not of a dearness and a death
But of a love turned ashes and breath
Gone out of beauty. . . .
. . . .
That April should be shattered by a ghost
That August should be levelled by a rain,
I can endure. . . .
. . . .
But that a dream can die, will be a thrust
Between my ribs forever of hot pain.

The poem, which was published four years later in a collection titled *The Harp-Weaver*, must certainly have been part of the coda to her affair with Arthur Ficke, the dazzlingly handsome poet for whom Millay seems to have felt a quality of love never equaled in any of her other relationships. The two had begun corresponding during the brouhaha over her *Lyric Year* submission, but they had never laid eyes on one another until Millay met the tall, dark, blue-eyed Midwesterner just as he was about to join Pershing's forces in 1918. The result of their meeting was a rapturous three-day affair from which Millay may never have quite recovered.

Ficke shipped off for Europe, where he remained for the final months of the war. It seems clear that Millay expected to resume their relationship when he returned, but for some reason—or perhaps for many—Ficke refused. He was married, and although he had been estranged from his wife, he was reluctant to divorce her, as she had been ill. But that alone cannot have been his reason for retreating from the relationship with Millay; he did, in fact, get a divorce after the war, and married an attractive artist named

Gladys Brown whom he had met in Europe. Millay's great nervous intensity may have overwhelmed Ficke as it did others; or he may have sensed in her hypersensitivity and tendency toward psychosomatic illnesses a potential scenario not too different from the one he wanted to leave behind; or perhaps he could not envision a relationship with a person of similar artistic temperament. In any case, in spite of his strong feelings for Millay, Ficke would not continue a sexual relationship with her, although the two remained intimate "spiritual friends" until his death in 1945.

More than two years after their first meeting, Millay wrote Ficke a letter which reveals how strong her attachment to him continued to be:

> Arthur,—
>
> I love you, too, my dear, and shall always, just as I did the first moment I saw you. You are a part of Loveliness to me.—Sometimes at night, when you were in France [during World War I], I would read over the sonnets you had sent me—just as you have been doing now with mine—and long for you in an anguish of sweet memory, and send all my spirit out to you in passion. It seemed incredible that you were not in the room with me. . . .
>
> . . . There are moments, of course, when I am with you, that is different. One's body, too, is lonely. And then, too, it is as if I knew of a swamp of violets, and wanted to take you there, and share them with you. . . .
>
> . . . You will never grow old to me, or die, or be lost in any way.
>
> —Vincent

Even long after it had become clear that she and Arthur would never be lovers again, Edna yearned to be

with him. Her feelings fluctuated widely between reckless passion and deep bitterness. In fact, the lovely title of her "serious" collection of poems, *Second April*, disguises Millay's pessimistic reaction to Ficke's failure to resume contact with her in the spring of 1919 after his return from the war. (It was the previous spring—the *first* April—which had brought the two face to face for the first time.) The original edition of *Second April* opened—revealingly, to those who knew about Edna and Arthur—with a short, bitter poem called "Spring," which contained these lines:

> It is apparent that there is no death.
> But what does that signify
> Not only under ground are the brains of men
> Eaten by maggots.
> Life in itself
> Is nothing,
> An empty cup, a flight of uncarpeted stairs.

Another poem in *Second April*, *"Passer Mortuus Est"* ("The Sparrow is Dead"), also opens with an image of despair:

> Death devours all lovely things:
> Lesbia with her sparrow
> Shares the darkness,—presently
> Every bed is narrow.

but at the final stanza hints at a resolution:

> After all, my erstwhile dear,
> My no longer cherished,
> Need we say it was not love,
> Just because it perished?

Here again is Millay's gift for giving poetic form to common experience—in this case, the internal alchemy by means of which we all survive our love affairs.

But although Millay may have succeeded in transmuting her passion for Ficke into a memory she could live with, the wound does seem never completely to have healed. Her exhaustion and confusion finally led Millay to flee her disorderly Greenwich Village existence for a while. Just after New Year's in 1921, she left for Paris. This was, of course, a very "twenties" thing to do; a period in Paris was de rigueur among young American artists. Scott Fitzgerald, Hemingway, e.e. cummings and many others were on their way, or already there. Millay's own reasons for going doubtless had something in common with theirs, but must also have included a desire to sort out her complex feelings for the men with whom she had been involved.

In Paris, though, Millay did not exactly get herself to a nunnery. Edmund Wilson, who also went there in 1921, found Edna "very much allied with the Bohemians of the Left Bank." They walked in the Bois de Bologne, and Edna asked Wilson to take her to southern France, claiming to be flat broke. Wilson declined because, he wrote later, "I knew that she was not to be relied upon and would leave me for anyone who seemed more attractive. I did not want to have to worry and suffer again."

Wilson's feelings may well have been justified; Millay was skilled at manipulating the people around her, especially men. In a letter to his friend, the poet John Peale Bishop (July 3, 1921), Wilson indicates that, in fact, Edna was living quite a high life in Paris, staying at a "first-rate hotel" and "better dressed . . . than she has ever been before

in her life." Wilson also told Bishop that Edna's health and spirits seemed good, that she looked "older, more mature" (she was then twenty-nine), and that "she was tired of breaking hearts and spreading havoc."

The two years spent in Europe were for Millay a pastiche of exuberance and depression, high drama and low comedy. She had fun, but there were black periods of despair, too, as her letters from Vienna during the winter of 1921-1922 reveal. The high times appear to have happened early in her European journey. "Le jazz hot" was sweeping Paris, and in a letter to "Hunk" (her sister Norma) of July, 1921, "Bincent"—Millay often used baby-talk in her letters to her family—gushes on and on about a jazz-party she attended.

> . . . that night I appeared in my most beautiful evening gown,—a Poiret gown, by the way, which I bought at a place where they sell the gowns which have been worn by the models—we all motored up to the Acacias and the jazz-band jazzed,—and Pete [Coggeshall, a friend of Norma Millay's] "took me on." Really, darling, it was a scream. . . . I had a hunch that they probably thought I couldn't dance very well, and I outdid myself, I've never danced more beautifully. It was too comical for anything.

That was Millay at her flapper best—bold, confident of her looks in a Poiret gown, defiant, unpredictable and wild. A few months later, her tone had changed. By October of 1921, Europe seemed a much grimmer place to Edna. For one thing, distance had not diminished her passion for Arthur Ficke—nor, apparently, his for her. She carried with her everywhere a large photograph he had sent her, and in a letter written from Albania in October, 1921, she apologized for having none to send him. "I will send you some snapshots," Edna promised, "as soon as I get them developed." In her letters, Edna's continuing anguish over not seeing Ficke is very apparent:

> Dear, when I come back to the States, won't you come east to see me? . . . I think we might have a few days together that would be entirely lovely. We are not children or fools, we are mad. And we of all people should be able to do the mad thing well. If each of us is afraid to see the other, that is only one more sympathy we have. If each of us is anguished lest we lose one another through some folly, then we are more deeply bound than any folly can undo.

There can be no doubt that Edna's feelings for Ficke were genuinely different from the emotions she felt in her many casual relationships with men. "I know what my heart wants of you," she wrote in the same letter of October, 1921, "it is not the things that other men can give." And she continued by reminding Ficke how much their desire for one another had influenced her poetry:

> Do you remember that poem in *Second April* which says, "Life is a quest and love a quarrel, Here is a place for me to lie!"?—That is what I want of you—out of the sight and sound of other people, to lie close to you and let the world rush by. To watch with you suns rising and moons rising in that purple edge outside most people's vision . . . .

What Edna wanted more than anything was not merely the excitement of sexual passion. Of that she had had plenty in Greenwich Village, and it only left her exhausted and lonely. Intimacy of a deeper, more complete sort was

what she sought with Arthur, a union of spirits between two gifted, creative persons who could see together what was "outside most people's vision." By implication, Millay recognized that her own gifts were complex and unusual, that what she required in a relationship would not easily fit the conventional patterns of interaction between a man and a woman. "You were the first man I ever kissed," Edna confessed, "without first thinking that I should be sorry about it afterwards. There has been only one other, a boy I truly loved, in a simpler way." Her letter ended with a desperate cry, "Arthur, it is wicked and useless,—all these months and months apart from you, all these years with only a glimpse of you in the face of everybody.—I tell you I must see you again."

From Rome, in November of 1921, Edna's letters to her mother and sisters remained chatty, full of Irish wit and nonsense. She promises "Normie" (her sister Norma) she will buy her some "long tortoise-shell earrings just as soon as the transportation strike"—there is always a transportation strike in Rome—"is over and it is possible to get a taxi." By early December, Millay had arrived in Vienna where, she wrote Arthur Ficke, she planned to stay for several months. "I am here because it is the cheapest place in the world to live just now, and I am in one of my periodic states of being entirely busted." In spite of her bright, upbeat correspondence with her family, the last line in this letter to Ficke (December 10, 1921) shows Edna's real state of mind: "It seems a long time since I have seen anybody I cared anything about."

While the days in Vienna passed, Edna's depression and loneliness grew. She had hoped to work on a novel,

Hardigut, while there; in fact, she had a contract with Horace Liveright for it. But her time in Vienna was not productive. Her moods shifted sharply, and in a single letter she would go from manic banter to anguished confessions of suffering. "Arthur, dearest," she wrote Ficke on January 24, 1922, "I feel quite gay and risible, having got all this pifflous bunk off my chest and onto yours. . . . Well, good-bye. I shall now issue forth and fodder my bewildered Muse on Wiener schnitzel, Brussel sprouts and beer." But after her signature, Edna added this line: "Write me and do not tear them up. For God's sake post them.—I am suffering in this place."

She really was suffering, and the pattern was hatefully familiar: a period of intense creativity and optimism followed by months of neurotic blackness which rendered her almost completely dysfunctional. In Vienna, Millay's Muse truly was "bewildered," if not becalmed. Evidence comes up in several letters, especially in two she wrote to the poet Witter ("Hal") Bynner. In the first (December 23, 1921) she wrote cryptically, "Dear Hal, there are thoughts in my head that I must not tell you now, particularly one of them. Because all this may not be true at all, may be just a dream that you had a month ago, and that I am having tonight.—Yet this I will say, that if it is a dream I am sorry." The dream, as it happened, was real: Bynner had proposed marriage, and Millay was inclined to accept. She wrote again to Bynner on January 23, 1922—just a month before her thirtieth birthday—that if his offer were still negotiable, she would accept it.

> You wrote me once, "we are too much alike, you and I, for any earthly marriage." I believe that to be

> nonsense .... Why it should be thought a good thing for people to spend their lives, which might otherwise not impossibly be used to some purpose, in a series of disagreements, misunderstandings, adjustments, ill-adjustments, I have never been able to see.

She explained, further, that her continuing love for Arthur Ficke should not deflect their plans. "I should not wish to marry Arthur," Edna protested, "even if it were possible." She admitted she would always love Ficke and said quite bluntly, "He is something to me that nobody else is." The very next day after writing Bynner, Millay wrote Ficke, sharing her plans to marry Hal. She was equally candid with Arthur:

> You, best of all, know how I feel about you, and always shall. No one can ever take your place with me. We know each other in such a terrible, certain, windless way. You and I have almost achieved that which is never achieved: we sit in each other's souls.

By April, Edna was back in Paris, where her spirits lightened appreciably. Her mother joined her in Europe, and the two spent the summer in the English countryside of Dorset Downs. Edna had arrived in England exhausted, suffering the effects of a severe cold, and much of her summer was spent recuperating. By this time Edna's plans for marrying Hal Bynner were up in the air—as they had been, indeed, since at least the beginning of March, when she wrote her sister Norma from Budapest,

> As for my getting married, I may and I may not. You know who this man is, Norma. At least you could guess. . . . Well, if you don't remember, you don't deserve to know. And if you do remember, don't breathe it to a soul.

On a less flippant level, though, Millay must have realized that she had very little control at that time over the outcome of any of her plans. While in England, she stayed just down the road from Gladys Brown, who was to marry Arthur Ficke in December of 1923. Her projected novel *Hardigut* was moving nowhere, though in a testy letter to Horace Liveright—"All this is a devilish nuisance"—she claimed "I have worked on the book in Vienna, and in Paris, and now in Dorset I am finishing it." (Millay abandoned the *Hardigut* project in 1923, for reasons of ill health.) And finally, Edna's marriage to Hal was off. She wrote Ficke from France on December 17, 1922: "As for Hal, there's not the slightest danger that I shall marry him: he has jilted me!" In the same letter she responded to Ficke's announcement that he intended to marry Gladys as soon as his divorce became final. "My God—it's marvelous," Edna enthused, " . . . And you didn't think we'd like each other!—men don't know very much."

Marvelous it may have been, but in the next paragraph Millay repeated what she had told Ficke so often: "I shall love you till the day I die.—Though I shan't always be thinking about it, thank God."

So there it all was at the end of 1922. None of Edna's plans had reached the fulfillment she expected. There was no novel for Liveright, no marriage to Hal, and Arthur Ficke was engaged to Gladys Brown.

Ironically, Millay's personal nadir at the end of that year was met by a stunning professional coup. It was announced that the Pulitzer Prize in Poetry for 1923 was to be hers in recognition of her achievements in *A Few Figs From Thistles* (expanded edition), eight sonnets from the

American Miscellany of Poetry for 1922, and "The Ballad of the Harp-Weaver," just published in pamphlet form by bookseller Frank Shay. So Edna returned to the States just after New Year's, 1923, her celebrity-status enhanced, her spirits depressed, her dreams unrealized, and her health miserable.

Esther Root, whom Edmund Wilson described to John Peale Bishop as "a large handsome unattractive rich amiable discontented girl," had attached herself to Edna in Europe, assuming the position of nurse/social secretary. Although Edna's old friends thought Root *too* protective, even possessive, she did serve a useful purpose during an especially difficult time. Millay was suffering intestinal disorders and could tolerate seeing very few visitors, though scores of invitations to speak poured in from across the country after her Pulitzer Prize was announced.

April of 1923 was the *sixth* April since Edna's brief, incandescent affair with Arthur Ficke. Though she had done almost no new work that winter, Edna was compiling a collection of poems —*The Harp-Weaver*—for a new publisher, Harper's. One weekend in April, Esther persuaded Edna to visit some friends they had met in Europe who were then staying in Croton, New York, and there she met "the solution" in the person of Eugen Boissevain, a Dutch coffee importer. Boissevain had been a widower since the death of Inez Mulholland, a Vassar alumna who had gained Millay's admiration as a feminist and social reformer. He and Millay had met twice previously with no particular effect, but this time each brought new needs to the encounter: Edna needed caring-for, and Eugen needed someone for whom to care.

By the end of May, 1923, Millay was writing to her mother,

> Darling, do you remember meeting Eugen Boissevain one day in Waverly Place?—It was only for a moment, and possibly you don't remember. But anyway, you will like him very much when you know him, which will be soon. And it is important that you should like him,—because I love him very much, I am going to marry him.
>
> *There* !!!!

Arthur Ficke must have known of Edna's nuptial plans. He and Gladys had been among the group of friends that met in Croton-on-the-Hudson that April weekend, and Arthur and Edna had been the ringleaders in staging an impromptu drama, a spoof on a current Broadway hit, with Boissevain and Millay featured as a couple of urban innocents who fall in love. As for Hal Bynner, we know that he and Edna remained friends, even after the abortive marriage scheme. Her letters to him—those which have survived and been published, at least—remain affectionate and lighthearted.

The "solution" was sealed on July 18, 1923, when Eugen and Edna were married at Croton-on-the-Hudson. There was no time for a honeymoon, for later that day Millay entered a hospital in New York City in order to undergo major surgery for her intestinal complications; while she was recuperating, Arthur Ficke corrected the page proofs of *The Harp-Weaver*. Work on the proofs continued through much of that summer, so Ficke and Edna saw a great deal of each other.

Death, despair, disease: these three specters haunt

much of Millay's poetry during the twenties. In spite of her dark images, however, Edna was pleased by what her poetry had achieved—not only the distinction of a Pulitzer Prize, but, at last, some financial recompense as well. Writing to her mother in November of 1923, a few months after her marriage to Boissevain and her surgery, Edna proudly noted that the bills she had recently settled for her mother had been paid *out of her own bank account*:

> . . . everybody thinks it is my rich husband who has done it, when in fact it is really I myself, every cent of it, with money that I made by writing,—nearly a thousand dollars, in all, since you went to Camden.
>
> Oh, well, it doesn't matter.

But indeed, it did matter to her considerably. In January of 1924, Edna set out alone on a lecture and poetry-reading tour that took her to places as diverse as Chicago and Cedar Rapids, Iowa. Her major motive was not devotion to art but, as she had told her mother, to make money: "My lecture trip in January and February will do wonders for me. I shall clear nearly two thousand dollars which will come in very handy." Edna wrote lively and amusing letters back to Boissevain in New York as she made her circuit around the Midwest. "I got through my two readings yesterday well enough," she wrote him from on board a train bound for Chicago, " . . . the one in the evening was in a private house!—A bunch of wealthy people came together to see what I looked like, and bet with each other how many of my naughty poems I would dare to read. . . . If ever I felt like a prostitute it was last night. —I kept saying over and over to myself while I was reading to them, 'Never mind—it's a hundred and fifty dollars.'—I hope I shall never write a poem again that more than five people will like."

Millay's "naughty" poems seem scarcely even colorful today, of course. In the twenties, however, they were something quite new: memoirs of a *woman's* frankly sexual feelings. Edna St. Vincent Millay had done something unprecedented in the tradition of English literature by introducing her intimate fantasies and feelings as themes of poetry. Certainly men (Shakespeare and Whitman are just two examples) had written of their own sexuality, but not women, whose thoughts about "love" were expected to be more lofty and explicitly moral. Then along came Millay's poetry, which was clearly not concerned with social conventions like fidelity ("Oh, think not I am faithful to a vow"), but with satisfaction of sensual desires ("After the feet of beauty fly my own").

In some of her poems, Millay seemed almost to celebrate what might easily be thought of as "promiscuity." One sonnet, for example, begins with these lines:

> What lips my lips have kissed, and where, and why,
> I have forgotten, and what arms have lain
> Under my head till morning. . . .

For a woman to speak easily of such experience, to introduce the telling physical detail which lends poetic authority, was a significant departure from the illusion of sexlessness which women for a long time had been expected to maintain. But although Millay's frankness was new, and a little shocking, it was not exploitative. When, in her later years, Harper Brothers wanted to bring out a volume called *The Love*

Poems of Edna St. Vincent Millay, with a foreword revealing the intimate details which lay behind the poems, Edna was appalled. She wrote, in a stinging letter of refusal:

> You state that, in your opinion, such a book as you describe would "make new readers" for me. I do not doubt it. People who never in all their lives, except when in school and under compulsion, have held a book of poems in their hands, might well be attracted by the erotic autobiography of a fairly conspicuous woman, even though she did write poetry. The indubitable fact that, even as I was winning very new readers, I should be losing entirely the good esteem of the more sensible and by me the most valued, of the readers I already have, does not seem to have occurred to you.

Millay's use of sensuality in her poetry was not decorative, or merely flamboyant. Love and death are the most potent themes of the poetic tradition, and the human body is the point where these themes converge; Millay recognized this, as so many poets have. Most of those poets, however, were men, and Millay was isolated by her gender from the very tradition which nurtured her poetry. Vincent Sheean remarked that "explicit passion on the part of a woman writer has been so completely unknown in English that it is no wonder this poet [Millay], indubitably born of this and no other language, had in her fire and tears to turn back to Greece." Millay had admired and grown to love the fragmentary poems that remain from the work of Sappho. (A bust of this Lesbian poet was, in fact, prominent in the living room of the Boissevains' house.) Sappho's lyrics, like Millay's, preferred the colloquial speech of everyday life, and they dwelt on the response of feelings and physical sensation to the world around her, including especially the beauty she saw in both men and women. The *experience* of passion is captured by Sappho in lines such as these:

> . . . elusive
> little flames play over the skin and smolder
> under. Eyes go blind in a flash. . . .

So too could Millay express in simple language the complex pleasures of sexual union:

> . . . the churning blood, the long
> Shuddering quiet, the desperate hot palms pressed
> Sharply together upon the escaping guest,
> The communion of souls unguarded, and grown strong.

Whether or not "Sapphic tendencies" were literally as well as poetically a part of Millay's life is impossible to know. It has been widely hinted that the psychological and physical delicacy which haunted Millay, particularly in later life, was partly due to the repression of conflicts about her sexual identity. Millay herself gave perhaps the best answer to this argument. Once at a cocktail party she was cornered by a psychoanalyst who inquired whether her health problems might not result from attraction to members of her own sex, and she is said to have retorted, "Oh, you mean I'm homosexual! Of course I am, and heterosexual, too; but what's that to do with my headache?"

The "headache" was to become Millay's constant companion for the rest of her life. "I've had a headache now for two months without an hour's respite, and dark spots before my eyes all the time," she wrote her mother in 1925. "If it isn't something else it damn well must be my eyes, for it's damn well something." Eugen Boissevain was to be-

come her nurse as well as her husband, managing all the affairs of their household and leaving Millay as free of stress as possible. He cooked, washed, dictated letters, and kept away unwanted visitors. "It is so obvious to anyone that Vincent is more important than I am," he is reported to have said once. "Anyone can buy and sell coffee . . . but anyone cannot write poetry."

Boissevain and Millay left New York in 1925 and moved to Steepletop, a scenic hundred-acre farm in the Berkshires. As the first quarter of the twentieth century closed, so too did the phase of Millay's life in which she was the epitome and expression of her age. The years to come were to be quite different from the ones which had gone before.

Millay's life and career as a poet seemed to continue unfolding in a predictable manner as the twenties drew to a close. Her poetry kept appearing with regularity in the "smart" magazines and in collections like *The Buck in the Snow* (1928). She had collaborated with composer Deems Taylor by writing the libretto for his opera *The King's Henchman*, produced very successfully in 1927 at New York's Metropolitan Opera. And Edna's public reading and lecturing continued, especially on college campuses, often to very enthusiastic audiences.

But there was, as well, a growing public and critical sentiment that Edna St. Vincent Millay's vogue was passing. *The Buck in the Snow*, the "harvest" of her first couple of years' work in the "shanty-studio" at Steepletop, was not well liked either by professional critics or by the loyal group of readers who had loved *A Few Figs from Thistles*. There were important exceptions, of course, among them Edmund Wilson, who wrote John Peale Bishop (October 17, 1928): "Have you seen Edna's new book—I think that the best things in it are wonderful. Her muse came to lately with a bang and she has already written almost enough for another work."

The publication of *The Buck in the Snow*, her last collection to appear in the 1920s, did, however, bring Millay a personal bonus—it gave her close and sustained contact with Arthur Ficke once more. Ficke and his wife Gladys came east from Santa Fe, where he had moved for reasons of health, to live with the Boissevains at Steepletop for several months in the spring of 1928. As he had with Edna's earlier collection, *The Harp-Weaver*, Ficke helped the poet proofread *The Buck*. In this new volume, too, there was at least one poem directly inspired by Edna's feelings for Arthur. Entitled "To The Wife of a Sick Friend," the poem is filled with beautifully haunting lines that express how protective Edna felt toward Arthur, whose health was extremely fragile at that time:

Shelter this candle. Shrewdly blowing
Down the cave from a secret door
Enters our only foe, the wind.
Hold it steady. Lest we stand,
Each in a sudden, separate dark,

. . . .

Alone, alone, in a terrible place,
In utter dark without a face,
With only the dripping of the water on the stone,
And the sound of your tears, and the taste of my own.

So many of Millay's earliest and most persistent images reappear in this lyric: the burning candle, her fear of confinement alone in "a terrible place," the darkness of caves, the dripping water. It must have been comforting when Arthur and Gladys Ficke decided to buy a property in the Berkshires just fourteen miles from Steepletop. "We shall never escape from each other," Edna had written Arthur in late October of 1920, shortly before she embarked for Europe. She was right.

Although Ficke was restored to her life, another kindred spirit, for whom Millay's feelings of intimate affection were almost equally strong, was lost forever.

On December 16, 1928, Elinor Wylie died suddenly at her home in New Canaan, Connecticut. Edna got the news just as she was about to walk out on stage to give a poetry reading at the Brooklyn Academy of Music. She was stunned, flattened by the news, and as she stepped onto the stage in a kind of trance, Edna began reciting, not her own lines, but Wylie's. Millay's improvised and grief-filled tribute was only the start of her slow coming-to-grips with Elinor's death. Not until ten years later did Edna's feelings about what had happened reach a fuller maturity in a brief series of six elegies, one of which begins:

> For you there is not song. . . .
> Only the shaking
> Of the voice that meant to sing; the sound of the strong
> Voice breaking.

From her earliest poems to her last ones, Millay tried to find images which would allow the dumb pain of mourning to speak to the reader. And as with her attempts to depict love, her poems about death and grief also center often on the realness of physical experience—the churning blood, the breaking voice.

With the close of the twenties, Millay's career, which had been so much a part of that decade, sputtered and then flattened out. She continued to write, but her work was regarded increasingly as that of a "major *minor* poet." Her role as America's premier female poetic voice was taken over by the likes of Marianne Moore and H.D., whose verses seemed closer to the revolutionary experiments in form, diction and imagery of men like Ezra Pound and T. S. Eliot. "Serious" literature became more and more identified with modernism, and Millay's work never fit into that mold. But with characteristic stubbornness, she refused to alter her own style, and found herself isolated from the mainstream of literature as well as of life.

Millay's ability—and need—to isolate herself was one of her strengths as a poet. In Camden, in Greenwich Village, at Steepletop, she survived the crushing pressures of the outside world—its narrowness, its ignorance of beauty, its loss of love—by pulling further inside herself to a world of the imagination. In a similar way, she could live a life of sexual freedom because she could—for the most part—take it all so impersonally and casually.

But if her spiritual isolation gave Millay a way to project an "alternative world" through poetry, it also intensified her anguish. Her endless physical problems and the grind of extreme emotional discomfort contributed also to the impression, already widespread among her friends in the twenties, that Edna was a "pathetic" creature. Her own

awareness of this impression must have been unendurably painful. Even in her moments of high success, such as the Met's production of *The King's Henchman*, Edna could collapse into an anxiety-ridden rubble. Edmund Wilson saw it happen at dinner the very evening of the Met's production, when an agitated Millay blurted out, "I'm not a pathetic figure—I'm not!" Wilson replied, "Whoever said you were?" and Edna's conversation suddenly careened in another direction: "I love life—I love every moment of it!—I love sitting here talking to you, having that sleet beating on the window."

Millay knew how erratic her emotions were, and some of her contemporaries, like Wilson, hinted that her marriage to Boissevain was a way to make herself a kind of "voluntary prisoner . . . . given up to other people's kind messes." This may very well have been true. Her marriage and subsequent withdrawal to Steepletop permitted Millay to "institutionalize" herself, with Eugen acting as a benign warden. Even Boissevain himself appears to have understood his role that way. When Edmund and Elena Wilson visited Steepletop in August of 1948, Eugen greeted them by saying "I'll go and get my child."

Certainly, alcoholism played some part in the diminishing of Millay's life. "I thought that she showed badly the effects of drinking," Edmund Wilson wrote, recalling his visit with her in 1948. "Her hands shook, and her chin flapped like an old woman. Gene kept drinking up about two-thirds of her drink, on the pretext of giving her a fresh one." There is ample evidence to suggest that Millay's drinking was a problem, from which Boissevain tried to protect her—in part by shielding her from the effects of the world, which were almost unendurably painful to her hypersensitive spirit. The old fear that the world would close in and crush her, the crucial image of her moving early poem "Renascence," constantly threatened Millay, and finally, in a sense, came true.

Yet through it all, Edna Millay retained her iridescent quality. She could change from moment to moment, shifting from the bleakest depression to the buoyant high spirits of her Greenwich Village days. Vincent Sheean's *The Indigo Bunting*, a lovely and appreciative memoir of Edna, describes two visits in the summer of 1945, when the Boissevains came from Steepletop to Bailey's Island, just off the coast of Maine. Of the first visit Sheean writes:

> Miss Millay was, to put it bluntly, a frightening apparition to many of us. Her temperament was so variable that it was impossible to tell what mood might overwhelm her next. . . . She had been going through a bad time. . . . I think the reason why even the most sympathetic stranger was frightened of Edna was that she was herself so terrified. Her terror communicated itself and created terror. . . .

At times like these, Sheean goes on to say, Edna had the capacity "to become so small and mouselike that one imagined she might actually vanish at any moment. Her green eyes departed; her body grew smaller; she was for the most part away."

Two months later the same group of friends met again. And this time, Millay was transfigured by a striking radiance. "Edna appeared at the top of the path," Sheean remembered, "and came swiftly down through the rocks, half running."

> She came toward us. . . . in a completely legendary manner, down through the anfractuous rocks, left and right and then straight forward, waving her arms at us and in spite of all this movement. . . . the sea gulls kept her company all the way, circling round and round. She had to jump from rock to rock in the last bit, over purling rivulets of sea water. . . .

When Edna reached her friends she appeared to be glowing with health and high spirits. "Her red hair was blown free," Sheean reported, "and her green eyes were gleaming." By this time Edna was in her early fifties, but she seemed as young as the laughing girl of twenty-five years earlier, turning the corner of Macdougal Street.

Above everything, Edna St. Vincent Millay was an honest analyst of love—neither sentimental nor cynical, always sensitive to passion but never blinded by it. Her finest poems express, with a clarity and simplicity that invite the reader to understand, the difficult balance of the heart.

> Love is not all: it is not meat or drink
> Nor slumber nor a roof against the rain;
> . . . .
> Love can not fill the thickened lung with breath,
> Nor clean the blood, nor set the fractured bone;
> Yet many a man is making friends with death
> Even as I speak, for lack of love alone.
> It well may be that in a difficult hour,
> . . . .
> I might be driven to sell your love for peace,
> Or take the memory of this night for food.
> It well may be. I do not think I would.

7

DOROTHY PARKER

"Brevity is the soul of lingerie—as the Petticoat said to the Chemise." In 1916, Dorothy Rothschild was learning the art of the one-liner by writing captions like this one for the photographs of luscious fashions which appeared in *Vogue.* This ten-dollar-a-week job was a school for conciseness from which Dorothy graduated with honors, to become one of the most devastating wits at the famous Algonquin Round Table. A remarkable writer, a keen observer of human foibles, and the virtuoso of the "drop dead" phrase, Dorothy Rothschild Parker became a legend even in her own day.

Parker is not much read now. Certainly she would come out poorly in any popularity contest with the likes of Fitzgerald and Hemingway—now considered the quintessential writers of the twenties. But she was, nevertheless, a brilliant writer, and deserving of far more attention than she presently gets. She was one of the inventors of the so-called *"New Yorker* story," and a sparkling practitioner of the slice-of-life genre; her "verse" (she declined to call it poetry) is probably as widely quoted as Shakespeare's. Her output was not great, of course—all of her good work fits into one fairly compact volume—and the fact that she never tackled the big works has almost certainly contributed to the fragility of her reputation. But, to an equal extent, her highly personal style and highly visible presence in the center of the "smart set" of the twenties have overpowered the small but excellent legacy of her writings.

In fact, Dorothy Parker herself was never quite committed to her identity as a writer, or at least never willing to make it her highest priority. Her love affairs, and the abundant night life that constantly beckoned, first in New York, then in Hollywood, drew much of her energy away from writing. Alcoholism—barely, and not always, under control throughout her life—made matters even worse. "I'm betraying my talent," she told a confidante in 1931, "I'm drinking, I'm not working. I have the most horrendous guilt."

Guilty or not, Dorothy Parker went her own way, fueled by a mixture of irresistible charm and vitriolic wit. At the height of her vogue, in the 1920s, those who knew Dorothy well were impressed—and sometimes annoyed—by her capacity to shift with dizzying speed from effusive affection to deadly malice. Edmund Wilson, who admired both Parker and her work, wrote that it was precisely "the conflicts in her nature" that made her interesting, far more interesting, he felt, than the other members of the Round Table. Playwright Lillian Hellman, who became a lifelong friend of Dorothy's after their first meeting in 1931, commented on the same thing, but more analytically. In her memoir *An Unfinished Woman,* Hellman spoke of Dorothy's love for playing the game of "embrace-denounce," of greeting a man or woman warmly, flatteringly, only to whisper as they left the room, "Did you ever meet such a shit?" This behavior, Hellman believed, "came from a desire to charm, to be loved, to be admired . . . . such desires brought self-contempt that could only be consoled by behind-the-back denunciations of almost comic violence."

The insatiable need to be loved: it was the dark force that motivated much of Dorothy Parker's behavior. With it went a need to be put down and punished as well, a need which she fulfilled in a series of love affairs with men who—although they never quite met her only-half-humorous criteria of being "handsome, reckless and stupid"—were nevertheless capable of causing her great unhappiness.

It may be true that Parker's rapier-like wit was the cutting edge of her own neurotic conflicts. A painful childhood and a dizzying career (in a time and place which were stressful to many other talents besides hers) certainly contributed to the tragic point of view which underlies her superficially amusing stories and poems. But it was not only the circumstances of her personal life which gave Parker's writing its grim vision; it was also her ability to observe, with unflinching acuity, the continuing miseries of the human condition—not the socioeconomic sort, but the kind we inflict on ourselves and each other in the struggle for emotional relief.

Dorothy Parker's stories and soliloquies still amuse and entertain; but they also illuminate, they discover *us,* what we hoped, did and didn't do, missed being, might dare to be. Perhaps that is why *The Portable Dorothy Parker*—which she herself assembled in 1944—has been printed and reprinted, revised and expanded, printed and reprinted again, and has gone on selling briskly for more than forty years. The ironies she exposed, the character defects she punctured, the tragicomic rhythms of "love" she ridiculed—these continue discovering us to ourselves.

The Algonquin Round Table had a curious—in fact, a silly—beginning, if the popular story is to be believed. In 1919, Dorothy Rothschild, Robert Benchley, and Robert E. Sherwood were among the group of "whiz kids" which perceptive editor Frank Crowninshield had assembled to produce *Vanity Fair* magazine. Benchley, at only twenty-eight, was managing editor; Dorothy, twenty-five, the drama critic; and Sherwood, the baby at twenty-three, was drama editor. Just down Forty-fourth Street from the *Vanity Fair* offices, a troop of midgets was performing at the Hippodrome. Every day when the three friends set out for lunch, Sherwood—a true giant of a man at six feet seven—was besieged by the midgets, who would sneak up behind him, grab him around the knees, and inquire about the weather "up there." One day, to avoid this nuisance, the trio ducked into the Algonquin for lunch—and there they continued to gather long after the midgets had moved on to other engagements.

For years before 1919, the Algonquin Hotel had catered to the whims and special interests of writers and

theatrical people; since its opening in 1902, the hotel, only a few steps from the Broadway theater district, had attracted such illustrious regular customers as the Barrymore family, Booth Tarkington and Douglas Fairbanks. Among these greats, a few budding writers and editors did not command immediate attention, and when the nucleus of what became the Round Table was formed, it was only a group of wisecrackers seated at a long side table. But by 1920, hotel owner Frank Case shrewdly moved his rapidly expanding group of literati from their side table in the Pergola Room to a large, round table in the center of the main dining room, which was to become the hottest spot in Manhattan.

The Round Table grew slowly at first, but before it wore itself out in the late twenties, the group included (among others) Franklin P. Adams (known popularly as F.P.A.), Alexander Woollcott, Harold Ross, Heywood Broun, Irving Berlin, George S. Kaufman, Marc Connelly and Herbert Bayard Swope. It was hardly what one would call a group of intellectual heavyweights—rather a bunch of wits who mostly devoted themselves to bantering and insulting one another. The early designation, "The Vicious Circle," was apt, since the members of the group seemed to thrive on insult and abuse, some of it charming perhaps, but in the cases of F.P.A. and Woollcott, often genuinely nasty.

To be a member of the Round Table, one had to be awfully quick on the uptake. "You could never play Lady MacBeth," Woollcott once informed actress Peggy Wood (an occasional member) at lunch. "No, Alex, but you could" was the immediate retort. On another occasion, one of the members made a snide comment about Marc Connelly's premature baldness: "Your head feels just like my wife's behind." "Yes," replied Connelly, "so it does."

Parker was not one of the group's more loquacious members, but when she did speak she usually managed to deliver somewhat more sparkling repartee than this kind of adolescent patter. In his memoirs, written in the late thirties, Algonquin owner Frank Case recalled that in the beginning she would make no attempt to keep up with the nonstop talkers. "She would simply sit, now and then saying something at which the others would laugh, and that was the end of it." No one would have guessed at the time that little "Dottie," as she was usually called, was one of the group's sharpest wits, or that her remarks were to be the most quoted and quotable to come from the assemblage. And certainly nobody would guess that Dottie would turn out to be the best writer of the lot. As for herself, in later years Parker was to scoff at the Round Table and her own contributions to it: "Dammit, it was the twenties, and we had to be smarty."

Still, Dorothy Parker is known today mostly for some of those Round Table wisecracks, a few snippets of poetry, and miscellaneous bon mots. (Almost anyone who remembers anything about her will recall, for example, that she was the author of the lines "Men seldom make passes/At girls who wear glasses.") From the very start it was a kind of malicious backhandedness that seemed to give Parker her zip. Unlike the boisterous and often vulgar Woollcott, Parker displayed a manner that was overly polite and gracious, with a polished finishing school manner covering up a kind of innate shyness, qualities which gave her witticisms, when they did come, an extra sting. It was an effect of intellectual whiplash. She was the absolute master of the

catty remark raised to literary perfection. Once, listening to praise of a certain woman at the Round Table, she intruded, in her usual whispering tones, "You know that woman speaks eighteen languages and can't say 'No' in any of them."

When the conversation turned to a certain actress who had fallen and broken a leg in London, Parker, in mock concern, added her lament: "Oh, how terrible, she must have done it sliding down a barrister." But slyness wasn't her only mode of attack; Parker didn't shy away from the direct insult. When it was reported to Dottie that President Coolidge was dead, her immediate response was "How could they tell?" And then there was her judgment of Katherine Hepburn's acting ability—this of Hepburn as a young ingénue—"She ran the gamut of emotions from A to B."

Apparently Parker's verbal wit was at its strongest when most spontaneous. Much of the humor around the Round Table was contrived and rehearsed, but when it came to rapid-fire ingenuity and inventiveness, Dottie could seldom be topped by her comrades. Once when playing word games she was asked to use the word "horticulture" in a sentence. Without batting an eye she replied: "You can lead a horticulture, but you can't make her think."

Stories like these, which are abundant, have made Parker seem almost inhuman, a theatrical figure created at the Algonquin and perpetuated on the pages of magazines. So powerful and complete does the Parker persona seem that it is hard to imagine a real woman behind it. But indeed such a woman did exist, and lived a life of brittle loneliness from beginning to end.

"All those writers who talk about their childhood," she mused in her later years. "Gentle God, if I ever wrote about mine, you wouldn't sit in the same room with me." Born in the seaside resort of West End, New Jersey, on August 22, 1893, Dorothy was the daughter of J. Henry Rothschild, a garment manufacturer in New York. Although Henry Rothschild was no relation to the famous European banking family, he was prosperous enough to afford a comfortable house on West Seventy-second Street in Manhattan, as well as the New Jersey summer place. There were servants and plenty of amenities, but not much in the way of affection, for Dorothy was an unwanted child, born nine years after her only sister. Her mother died while Dorothy was still an infant, and her father had little or no interest in his belated daughter.

Rothschild was seemingly a parent of the "children should be seen and not heard" variety, and his only concern was that Dorothy learn proper deportment. Dinner was promptly at 6:30, and if Dorothy wasn't silently at her place at that exact hour her father would rap her wrist with a spoon. Of conversation at the table there was none—at least none for Dorothy. Her early school days, which began at a school run by the Nuns of the Blessed Sacrament, were not much more comforting. Dorothy, being half-Jewish, was treated as something of an alien or outsider; she had no friends at the school, and would make none, although records show she was a reasonably good student.

It was not until she reached high school age, and was packed off to Miss Dana's School in Morristown, New Jersey, that things looked up a bit. Miss Dana's School was a top-notch place academically—although it was what

many people in those days contemptuously referred to as a "finishing school." Dorothy was at least no longer hemmed in by the murky and unintelligible theology of Blessed Sacrament School. Miss Dana's curriculum was challenging, and when Dorothy graduated she had the foundations of a very fine education, including instruction in Latin, math, the sciences, all the arts. The school put special emphasis on the speaking voice and elocution, and here it was that Dorothy began not only to read poetry, but to write it as well. Her secondary education was easily the equivalent of a college education in the liberal arts today.

It was typical of Dorothy in later years to refer to herself as a stringy-haired ugly duckling, a proverbial bad girl and rebel, but the testimony of those who remembered her says otherwise. Parker's biographer John Keats located one of Dorothy's former classmates, who testified that the young Dorothy Rothschild was quite attractive. "She was small, slender, dark-haired and brilliant. . . . I admired her as being an attractive girl; she was peppy and she was never bored. She was outstanding in school work, but I can't remember her playing any games." There was a good deal of social, as well as intellectual, training at Miss Dana's, and apparently this too stuck, for Dorothy came out of the system with flawless manners and a lady-like demeanor.

In pre-World War I America, a girls' finishing school was just that: a place where a woman's education was finished, ended. In those days college was considered by many a social indiscretion for daughters of the rich—a sign perhaps that a girl was trying to be useful rather than ornamental. In the view of Mr. Henry Rothschild, Dorothy's only acceptable alternative on leaving school was to sit home and wait for the appropriate husband to come along. But alas, the right man did not immediately appear, and as fortune would have it, the year after her graduation from Miss Dana's, Dorothy's father died. She was completely on her own, without any kind of financial support, and so Dorothy took a step that led even more certainly than college into social oblivion: she went to work. Since she was not prepared for anything in particular, the next few years of her life were desperate ones of picking up whatever low-paying lady-like work she could get. For a while she supported herself by playing the piano in a dancing school for a few days a week.

During the period before World War I, and before Dorothy's literary career began in earnest, she lived for several years in a boarding house at 103rd Street and Broadway, paying eight dollars a week for a room with two meals a day. It was an arrangement that no respectable woman of her social set would have abided, but Dorothy had evidently reached the conclusion that whatever her destiny, she had to search it out for herself on the urban stage of Gotham. She made a wholly new bunch of friends, and quite luckily her own boarding house had the right sort of people. Her first literary acquaintance was made here; it was with Thorn Smith, who later became extremely popular for his fantastic and ribald books such as *Night Life of the Gods, Topper Takes a Trip* and others which were made into successful movies in the early thirties. Dottie spent many of her evenings chatting with Thorn Smith and another boarder. "There was no money, but Jesus we had fun," she recalled long afterwards.

Dorothy's life from 1911 to 1916 has left few traces,

and she never wanted to talk much about that time in later years. In 1916, one of her verses was accepted by *Vogue,* and this proved the beginning of her career. She received only twelve dollars for her contribution, but Frank Crowninshield's remarkable nose for talent must have twitched when he came across the little poem, for shortly after accepting the verse, Crowninshield called her in for an interview and ended up offering Dorothy a job at *Vogue.* In truth, this first break probably came as much because of her appearance as because of her talent; *Vogue* was then, as now, a magazine of expensive fashions, and Dorothy was an expensive and fashionable dresser. All her life, no matter how dire her economic condition was, she never scrimped on clothes—or indeed, on much of anything else.

Dottie's stint on *Vogue* was to be a short one, however, for soon afterward Frank Crowninshield transferred her to another of his magazines, one that was both dearer to his heart and more neatly tailored to Dorothy Rothschild's talents—*Vanity Fair.* In essence, *Vanity Fair* was a "smart magazine," like *Judge,* the old *Life* and *The Smart Set*—like the *New Yorker* was to be in its first few years. In theory the magazine was aimed at rich city sophisticates. When Condé Nast first started the magazine in 1913, it was a kind of imitation *Vogue.* It was then even called *Dress and Vanity Fair.* But when Nast showed a copy of the magazine to his old friend Crowninshield, the latter made the instant suggestion that what was needed in New York was a magazine dealing with "what people talk about at parties—the arts, sports, humor, and so forth." Crowninshield was made the editor, and developed a magazine along these lines. In an interview some thirty years later for a *New*

Yorker profile, Crowninshield analyzed the motives which gave rise to the style of *Vanity Fair:* "My interest in Society —at times so pronounced that the word 'snob' comes to mind—derives from the fact that I like an immense number of things which society, money and position bring in their train: paintings, tapestries, rare books, smart dresses, dances, gardens, country houses, correct cuisine, pretty women."

All very slick, very superficial one might suppose, but a magazine like *Vanity Fair* could be, as *The Smart Set* was for H. L. Mencken and George Jean Nathan, an excellent showplace for young writers. And it wasn't long before a number of up-and-coming talents were appearing in the magazine. In the years after the war, *Vanity Fair* not only had Benchley, Parker and Sherwood on its staff, it also displayed the diverse talents of Edmund Wilson, Alexander Woollcott, Aldous Huxley, Gertrude Stein, e.e. cummings, Edna St. Vincent Millay, Elinor Wylie, Paul Gallico and Grantland Rice. The magazine featured the photographs of Edward Steichen and Cecil Beaton; it was open to the drama (Dorothy Parker soon became the magazine's drama critic), even the movies (Gilbert Seldes and Robert E. Sherwood carved out a completely new form—movie criticism); and many Americans heard for the first time, in the pages of *Vanity Fair,* of some of the great artists of the twentieth century—Picasso, Matisse, Rouault, Gauguin.

In 1917, the year the United States entered World War I, Dorothy Rothschild not only began her work on *Vanity Fair,* she also married the man whose name she would bear for the rest of her life: Edwin Pond Parker, II, the young scion of a Hartford, Connecticut family, who was just beginning a Wall Street career. In later years Dottie

joked that she had married Parker to change her name, but the obvious truth, to all who knew the young couple, was that the two were very much in love, at least in the beginning. Parker was tall, handsome, charming and well-heeled —the very sort of young man any mother would want for her daughter, or so it seemed.

In fact, however, Eddie Parker was an alcoholic, as Dorothy began to realize during the first year of her marriage. Eddie volunteered when America entered World War I, and he was subsequently stationed at several military camps in the East. Dorothy religiously followed her new husband around on weekend visits until he was shipped out near the war's end, and during these visits, Dorothy found that Eddie would often polish off a whole bottle of something and pass out in a stupor. His army buddies named him "Spook" because he would show up for reveille pale as a ghost and still drunk. Dorothy herself, of course, was no amateur at drinking, and it may well be that she, like many budding alcoholics, sought out a full-blown case for a marriage partner.

But Eddie's alcoholism was not, perhaps, so important a factor in the disintegration of their marriage as was his personality—by all accounts pleasant, but undistinguished. After the war he predictably rejoined his old Wall Street firm, resuming a way of life and a point of view which were at quite a distance from those of the "smart set" to which Dorothy by now belonged. For a while he occasionally attended luncheons at the Algonquin, but although he was liked well enough, he never quite fit in, and eventually stopped coming. At first, although Eddie was no longer being seen at the Algonquin, he was still heard about.

Dorothy would bring him up regularly in the conversation, mostly as the victim of some misfortune. When one of the regulars of the group asked where Eddie was, Dorothy would invariably have an excruciatingly funny story about his daily mishap—falling in a manhole, getting his arm stuck in some machinery, or whatever. And so it was that the fate of the real Eddie became obscured by a cloud of witty invention, setting a pattern for the rest of Dorothy's emotional life.

The Parker marriage was not legally dissolved until 1928, but for practical purposes, Eddie had vanished from Dorothy's life before 1922. The effect of this loss is really impossible to determine, for Dorothy Parker was not very analytical about herself or very forthcoming about her feelings. But it seems clear that the failure of her relationship with Eddie Parker had a serious impact on Dorothy. All of her relationships with men, and close friends of either sex, were to be guarded and uneasy in the future. Wit, the barbed tongue were to become defense mechanisms against the expected tragedy of intimacy. The breakup of her marriage seems to have re-emphasized for Dorothy the essential loneliness and isolation of the human condition.

Lunch at the Algonquin offered the only kind of social intimacy Dorothy really found comfortable: the company was close and amusing, but its demands vanished when the meal ended and each Algonquinite returned to his or her "private world." Dorothy's appearance at the Round Table gatherings was always memorable, not only for what she said but for how she looked as well. Her small, wistful facial features were accentuated by the way she wore her hair, parted and then combed down in a kind of curtain-opening

for her enormous eyes. Her voice had that "finishing school" refinement, soft, a little breathy, demure. Often she wore an unruly feather boa that made its way regularly into other people's plates or was set afire by their cigarettes. (It was said Dorothy had the only boa in the world that actually molted.) Her clothes were chic, often quite expensive, but they somehow looked incongruous on her tiny frame. Even in her late twenties, Dorothy could have passed as a child; she was the kind of woman who looked so vulnerable and helpless that you wanted to take her in your arms, dry her tears and comfort her.

But Parker needed protection about as much as a hornet does. Her marriage to Eddie had not only awakened her to the dangers of intimacy, it had hardened her as well. That marriage—amounting, really, to a few weekends together over a nine-month period, followed by letters to an absent husband—had cured Dorothy of romance, or at least of the romantic expectations the young often seek in relationships.

By 1920, Dorothy Parker had reached an odd plateau. She was married, but effectively had no husband. She was one of the most quoted women in New York, but she was unemployed.

Parker had gotten herself fired from *Vanity Fair* by writing such scathing drama reviews that powerful members of the theatrical community—like Billie Burke, who was then married to Florenz Ziegfield—had become enraged. But she didn't remain idle for long. Free-lancing it for awhile, she and Robert Benchley rented a minuscule office on the third floor of the Metropolitan Opera House studios. According to legend, their shingle read, "Utica

Drop Forge and Tool Co., Robert Benchley, President; Dorothy Parker, President." The free-lance period was brief for Benchley, who had a wife and three small children to support. Dorothy kept at it for awhile, in 1920 and 1921, though not even her best friends could understand how she survived financially. When she went out—which was often—there was never any money for the taxi or the drinks, though she continued buying expensive perfume, handmade lingerie, and designer dresses. She had evidently taken to heart Oscar Wilde's aphorism, "Take care of the luxuries and the necessities will take care of themselves."

However precarious her finances may have been at this juncture, uncertainty did nothing to diminish her outrageous wit or manner of living. Her bon mots acquired the status of legend:

> *Dorothy* (at a Halloween party): "What are those people doing around the washtub?"
> *Reply:* "They're ducking for apples."
> *Dorothy* (sighing): "There, but for a typographical error, is the story of my life."

At her cheaply furnished apartment on West Fifty-seventh Street, she kept a canary which she called "Onan," because, as she gravely explained, he spilled his seed upon the ground.

Always, there were rumors of love affairs. Dorothy and Robert Benchley were linked by an imaginative gossip columnist, though there was no substance to the rumor. Men did enter her life, however, and one of these—the most important—was Charles MacArthur, with whom Dorothy fell in love in 1922. MacArthur was

without a doubt enormously attractive; tall and talented, he was a Round Table regular, a newspaper journalist, and (his male friends knew) a notorious womanizer. Despite the unhappiness of her marriage to Edwin Parker—and in spite of her cynical attitude toward the exaltation of "romance"—Dorothy appears to have fallen desperately for MacArthur. "Charley was marvelous," Dorothy's friend Donald Ogden Stewart later said. "He was something all his own, and she was so in love it was really a serious, desperate thing. When Dottie fell in love, my God, it was really the works. She was madly in love. She was not a slave to love, exactly; it was really for keeps. She fell in love so deeply: she was wide open to Charley."

The vivid Parker/MacArthur affair soon fell victim, however, to the personalities of the two protagonists. Charley continued to "sleep around" even during their involvement, and this was unendurable to the already bruised Dorothy. To make matters far worse, Dorothy discovered she was pregnant, though her friends were not sure by whom. The abortion which followed, although she undertook it without hesitation, was brutally traumatic—or so one assumes from the events which followed, for shortly after her hospitalization, Parker attempted suicide in the bathroom of her apartment by slashing her wrists with a razor which had belonged to the vanished Eddie.

In typical twenties fashion, Dorothy tried to brush off the whole business with hard-boiled humor. She tied gay blue ribbons on her bandaged wrists and joked that "Spook" hadn't even kept his razors sharp. But her friends were genuinely alarmed by the obvious signs of mental instability. Dorothy's black humor could not change the fact that she had suffered three devastating emotional crises: the loss of MacArthur (who married Helen Hayes), an abortion, and a suicidal episode—all in the space of a year.

She was now thirty years old; her finances were a shambles, her marriage had failed, and although her reputation as a writer of fiction in the smart magazines was growing, she had not yet published a serious work of poetry or prose. In the same year that Dorothy Parker attempted suicide, Edna St. Vincent Millay, only a year older than Parker, received the Pulitzer Prize.

But Dorothy Parker was a survivor. After her hospitalization she resumed the hectic social life that characterized the Algonquin circle. Like most of the other members of that group, Dorothy rarely began her day before noon, when she and her friends gathered for lunch. After that, there might be an impromptu afternoon amusement—a carriage ride along Fifth Avenue—or a bit of work. Late afternoons brought visits to one of several favorite speakeasies on the West Side. Of these establishments, the Algonquin crowd favored Jack and Charley's Puncheon Club, 42 West Forty-ninth Street. Unlike most other Prohibition-era bars, Jack and Charley's served *good* liquor *and* good food. More importantly, perhaps, the Puncheon Club had glitter, panache—it was the place to be seen. By 1924 the club had moved to 21 West Forty-ninth, where it became known simply as the "21."

And, of course, there were parties. The Round Table coterie often gathered, after supper and the theater,

at the studio of painter Neysa McMein, where the likes of George Gershwin and Ethel Barrymore also convened. From McMein's studio, Dorothy and her friends would often move on to Polly Adler's for breakfast. Mrs. Adler operated a very respectable bordello which, in addition to providing what bordellos usually provide, served up fine food, good conversation and the occasional game of backgammon.

If all this seemed to reflect a life style of the effete rich, it did so with good reason: many of the Algonquinites came from privileged backgrounds. Dorothy, in spite of her childhood miseries, had been raised to expect the finer things as her rightful due, and lack of money did not, in her view, require a retreat from luxury. If she couldn't pay—for taxis, drinks, dinners—others would, gladly. Besides, even when Dorothy made money—lots of it, as she did in Hollywood in the thirties—she could never keep track of it. It was not at all uncommon for Parker to blow into New York from some distant city, put herself up at an expensive suite in the Plaza, and then call friends to announce that she was in town without a penny to her name. Literally. No one ever figured out quite how she did it.

In the twenties, Dorothy scarcely had a reputation as a workaholic. When she did work—as rarely as possible —she hit hard at her writing, carefully choosing her words and polishing her style; in that sense, Parker was a dyed-in-the-wool perfectionist. On the whole, however, she preferred the "21" and Polly's to evenings in front of her portable typewriter. Quite simply, being a member of the sophisticated set to which Parker belonged was itself a kind of full-time occupation. While Dorothy might have thought of herself as a "working girl," her actual life bore little resemblance to that of the countless shopgirls, telephone operators, clerks and cleaning ladies who trudged off to low-paying jobs every morning.

But although Dorothy Parker lived the nineteen-twenties version of the "good life," she did not always—or even, perhaps, very often—have a good time. The stories she wrote revealed a sharp sense of the triviality of sophisticated city life, and a dark vision of the shallowness, even cruelty which characterized most social relationships. She herself was both a victim and a perpetrator. In a deep-seated way, Parker disapproved of her own participation in this hollow life, but she never seemed able to extricate herself, or even to try. Instead, she wrote about it.

Those who knew and admired her writing—like the irascible critic and journalist Alexander Woollcott—admitted that Parker invented out of pure imagination very few of the characters or situations in her fiction. Her stories truly were slices of life—cut out, often painfully, from her own experiences. Take Parker's "Lady with a Lamp," for instance. The story is a monologue by a chatty, brainless "friend" who visits "Mona," a young woman in bed with a mysterious "illness." It becomes clear as the story unfolds that Mona has had a disastrous affair with a married man, that she has gotten pregnant and had an abortion. Her nerves are shot, she is confused and traumatized, but her "friend" chatters on, saying all the wrong things:

> What doctor did you have, darling? Or don't you want to say? Your own? Your own Doctor Britton? You don't mean it! Well, I certainly never thought he would do a thing like—Yes, dear, of course he's

a nerve specialist. Yes, dear. Yes, dear. Yes, dear, of course you have perfect confidence in him. I only wish you would in me, once in a while; after we went to school together and everything. You might know I absolutely sympathize with you. I don't see how you could possibly have done anything else, I know you've always talked about how you'd give anything to have a baby, but it would have been so terribly unfair to bring it into the world without being married. You'd have to go live abroad and never see anybody and—. . . . Mona, for heaven's sake! Don't scream like that. I'm not deaf you know. All right, dear, all right, all right, all right. . . .

One can't help laughing at Mona's "friend," but the story is actually brutal, and one which Dorothy Parker scarcely had to dream up in order to write about. In a lighter vein is Parker's wicked parody of New York's sophisticated "high society," a story entitled "From the Diary of a New York Lady" and subtitled "During Days of Horror, Despair and World Change." A sample entry:

Wednesday. The most terrible thing happened *just this minute.* Broke one of my finger nails *right off short.* Absolutely *the* most horrible thing I ever had happen to me in my life. Called up Miss Rose to come over and shape it for me, but she was out for the day. I have *the* worst luck in the *entire* world. . . . *Damn* Miss Rose. . . .

And on "Thursday":

Simply *collapsing* on my feet. Last night *too* marvelous. "Everybody Up" *too* divine, *couldn't* be filthier, and the new number was there, *too* celestial, only he didn't see me. He was with Florence Keeler in the *loathsome* gold Schiaparelli model of hers that every *shopgirl* has had since *God* knows. . . .

And again on "Friday":

> Absolutely *sunk; couldn't* be worse. Last night *too* divine, movie *simply* deadly. Took Ollie to the Kingsland's party, *too* unbelievable, everybody absolutely *rolling.* They had those Hungarians in the green coats, but Stevie Hunter wasn't there. He's got a *complete* nervous breakdown. Worried *sick* for fear he won't be well by tonight; will absolutely *never* forgive him if he doesn't come. . . . Every time I look at those *revolting* black nails, I want to absolutely *yip.* I really have the most horrible things happen to me of anybody in the *entire* world. *Damn* Miss Rose.

What's a girl to do? Again, it's funny stuff, but there's venom underneath. By 1925, Dorothy Parker had come to hate the life she led, though at another level she wouldn't have traded it for anything in the world. Torn between the "fun of it all" and a growing sense of abject futility, Parker poured her contempt—of her glitzy New York world, of herself—into bitter, clever fiction.

Still, sometimes, the reality of her unhappiness caught up with Parker. There was a second suicide attempt, this time with sleeping pills. By now, Dorothy's friends could not share in the cheerful badinage with which she tried to dismiss the insanity of her behavior. "If you realized how repulsive you looked," Robert Benchley stormed at her, "you'd never try this again. You were a mess. You were lying there drooling, and if you had any consideration for your friends, you'd shoot yourself—but don't be this messy."

As Benchley's frustrated outburst suggests, Dorothy Parker was an *extremely* trying friend. Although she could be so charming that it was almost impossible not to be captivated by her, she could also be spectacularly destructive.

Her moods changed often and violently, from the insouciance of Jack and Charlie's "21" to suicidal depression. Too, the stinging wit that she habitually used to shield her feelings could strike even close friends as cold cruelty. Edmund Wilson, for example, was stunned when he informed Dorothy that "a former lover of hers had died, a young good-looking and well-to-do fellow who had suffered from tuberculosis," whereupon Parker crisply replied, "I don't see what else he could have done."

Another continuing source of annoyance, and even despair, for Dorothy's caring friends was her determination to involve herself in romances which took a great deal out of her emotionally and seemed to return little in the way of happiness. Typical was her affair with Seward Collins. Collins was very rich, heir to a chain of tobacco stores that stretched across the United States; he was also a prominent supporter of American literature, editor of *The Bookman,* a prestigious journal that regularly published work by new authors. Dorothy accompanied Collins on a trip to Europe in the summer of 1926, but the holiday did not, by any means, cement their relationship. They quarreled constantly, and after an excursion to Spain, where Dorothy became hysterical at the sight of a horse being gored by a bull and Seward was almost arrested for allegedly insulting a minor railway official, they returned to Paris, where Parker sent Collins back to the States. Later in her life, Dorothy dismissed the whole affair with a succinct comment: "I ran off to the Riviera with a Trotskyite."

By the time Dorothy got back to New York in the fall of 1926, her first book of poetry, *Enough Rope,* was just appearing. Boni and Liveright were her publishers, and both they and she began reaping huge profits from its sales. Like

Edna Millay's *A Few Figs from Thistles* (1920), *Enough Rope* became an instant and provocative best seller. The mood of Parker's poems was cynical, sardonic, saved from downright grimness only by their off-handed manner and verbal dexterity. Men, she seemed to say, were preternaturally fickle, love was a game of dishonest rules, of deceit, but still worth playing because in this world of hypocrisy there isn't anything better. The Dorothy Parker trademark appeared boldly in *Enough Rope:* the whiplash ending to a poem, that extra crack of hurt that makes the lesson smart and linger. What makes this jolt so gripping and effective is that it is natural, uncontrived; it is the poet administering the blow to herself. Here is vintage Dorothy Parker in "Symptom Recital":

I do not like my state of mind;
I'm bitter, querulous, unkind.
I hate my legs, I hate my hands,
I do not yearn for lovelier lands.
I dread the dawn's recurrent light;
I hate to go to bed at night.
I snoot at simple earnest folk.
I cannot take the gentlest joke.
I find no peace in pain or type.
My world is but a lot of tripe.
I'm disillusioned, empty-breasted.
For what I think, I'd be arrested.
I am not sick, I am not well.
My quondam dreams are shot to hell.
My soul is crushed, my spirit sore;
I do not like me anymore.
I cavil, quarrel, grumble, grouse,
I ponder on the narrow house.
I shudder at the thought of men. . . .
I'm due to fall in love again.

On the fickleness and unreliability of men, Dorothy Parker remains the quintessential poetic *grande dame.* The theme gave her some of her most pungent and memorable lines in *Enough Rope.* Here she is in "De Profundis":

> Oh, is it, then, Utopian
> To hope that I might meet a man
> Who'll not relate in accents suave,
> The tales of girls he used to have?

And in "Experience":

> Some men break your heart in two,
> Some men fawn and flatter,
> Some men never look at you;
> And that cleans up the matter.

More often than not, Parker's mood is one of despair, sometimes disgust, with just a streak of sunshine peeping through, a brief note of unhappy jollity. Here she is in "General Review of the Sex Situation":

> Woman wants monogamy;
> Man delights in novelty,
> Love is woman's moon and sun;
> Man has other forms of fun.
> Woman lives but in her lord;
> Count to ten and man is bored.
> With this the gist and sum of it,
> What earthly good can come of it?

The ending a question, not a statement—always the lingering hope that something good can come of the relation between the sexes because, however flawed and imperfect, there's little else.

Critical reactions to *Enough Rope* were positive but

somewhat patronizing. Genevieve Taggard of *The New York Herald-Tribune* epitomized the tone of many reviewers when, contrasting Parker's work to Millay's "superior" lyrics, she wrote that the poems of *Enough Rope* were "whiskey straight, not champagne." Parker would have loved the comparison, but her closest friends from the Round Table, like Alexander Woollcott, were furious that her poetry was being treated as merely 'light' verse—frothy, insubstantial, and ultimately not of lasting importance. Woollcott felt, though his was a minority opinion, that a substantial portion of Parker's collection was "thrilling poetry of a piercing and rueful beauty."

Thrilling or not, Dorothy's poems made money—a welcome event in view of her perpetually problematic finances and her recent rupture with the wealthy Seward Collins. Her flamboyant life style was, after all, a costly one. And not merely in terms of money.

Among the Algonquinites, of course, drinking was an honorable profession, and the ability to hold one's liquor well was especially prized. But Dorothy had gone beyond the social dimension of drinking. By the late twenties, when she was in her mid-thirties, Dorothy had developed the habit of drinking whiskey sours at breakfast and of nipping throughout the rest of the day. She may not have been "falling down drunk," but she was rarely sober, either. Her strategy, a common one among alcoholics, was to drink relatively little *in public*; she simply made sure she arrived at a party already well oiled.

Here again, the best gloss on Parker's own life is to be found in her stories. "Big Blonde" perhaps Parker's most enduring—certainly most frequently reprinted—story,

seems to tell something of Parker's own relationship to alcohol. Hazel Morse, the "Big Blonde," is a jovial, large-boned woman who seemed in her youth to live for the good times alone. Attractiveness, popularity, "being liked" were her gods—and she was well-endowed with charm of a superficial variety, of the kind which arrests the attention of men who "click their tongues and wag their heads roguishly," the traveling salesman, perhaps, or the water-cooler Lothario.

Eventually Hazel finds herself trapped in a series of meaningless marriages that grow stale—stale because there is nothing to back them up, because good times, hilarity, can only be sustained by the physical zest of youth. Above all, in an age of speakeasies, of uproariousness, of superficial glitter, it becomes obvious that city life, once you get below the surface is empty and hollow; there is no true civilization to back it up—no kindness, no gentility, no sense of commonality of life, no roots.

To ease the utter boredom of her life, Hazel Morse takes to whiskey:

> She could not recall the definite day that she started drinking, herself. There was nothing separate about her days. Like drops upon a window pane, they ran together and trickled away. . . .
>
> She had never needed to drink, formerly. . . . If she took a cocktail, it was so unusual as to cause twenty minutes or so of jocular comment. But now the anguish was in her. . . .
>
> She hated the taste of liquor. Gin, plain or in mixtures, made her promptly sick. After experiment, she found that Scotch whiskey was best for her. She took it without water, because that was the quickest way to its effect.

But eventually, drinking doesn't seem to do the trick for Hazel anymore.

> She slept, aided by whiskey, till deep in the afternoons, then lay abed, a bottle and a glass at her hand, until it was time to dress and go out for dinner. She was beginning to feel toward alcohol a little puzzled distrust, as toward an old friend who has refused a simple favor. Whiskey could still soothe her most of the time, but there were sudden, inexplicable moments when the cloud fell treacherously away from her, and she was sawed by the sorrow and bewilderment and nuisance of all living.

The "Big Blonde" is one of those homeless waifs, so characteristically American, thrown out on a society that is unknowing and uncaring even with all its affluence. Hazel Morse flounders against all odds to capture some feeling of humanity. She is a figure of tragic dimensions, not unlike those floating and bobbing social outcasts found so fully developed in the novels of Theodore Dreiser—characters like Sister Carrie, Jennie Gerhardt and Clyde Griffiths.

Unquestionably, Dorothy Parker knew the type well. And while she herself maintained the cultural and personal reserves to avoid the fate of her hapless character, it was her own feeling of alienation, her own essential loneliness in New York, that gave her the artistic eye to penetrate the depths of this tragic character. Parker may have been Queen of the Round Table, its chief wit and wisecracker, but she never had any faith that their vivid world of cocktail parties, of bonhomie, could endure or that it had any depth to begin with. She was always aware that the shining and brittle surface of things was poised, ready

to fall through, that fun and good times could not endure, would not endure, in spite of all life's energies that were committed to keeping them bolstered up.

Indeed, by the end of the twenties, the old crowd at the Algonquin Round Table was dissolving. The "Vicious Circle" was proving too much even for those who enjoyed rehearsed invective and self-dramatizing humor. Robert Benchley had abandoned the group, and by 1927 Dorothy Parker was one of the few remaining Algonquin "originals." By now, the Algonquinites had themselves become the object of wicked parodies. In 1927 Anita Loos had written a sequel to *Gentlemen Prefer Blondes* entitled *But Gentlemen Marry Brunettes*, which contained a clever parody of the goings-on at the Round Table. Miss Loos's heroine says:

> So then they all started to tell about a famous trip they took to Europe. And they had a marvelous time, because everywhere they went, they would sit in the hotel, and play cute games and tell reminiscences about the Algonquin. And I think it is wonderful to have so many internal resources that you never have to bother to go outside yourself to see anything. . . . And I really do not know why the geniuses at the Algonquin should bother to learn about Europe any more than Europe bothers to learn about them. So they came back, because they like the Algonquin best after all. And I think it is remarkable, because the old Proverb tells about the Prophet who is without honor in his own home. But with them, it is just the reverse.

Anita Loos had drawn a bead squarely on the Round Table's soft underbelly: its provincialism disguised as cosmopolitan urbanity, its self-absorption masquerading as chic worldliness. And truth to tell, Parker herself was often contemptuous of the Algonquin's works and pomps, though she had a talent for concealing her contempt from those to whom she chose not to reveal it.

Indeed, hardly anyone knew Dorothy's thoughts and feelings about anything. Her great skill was to get other people to talk about themselves, never giving anything of her own away. This strategy worked so well that Parker was considered an exceptionally engaging conversationalist, even though she said relatively little. By some almost magical process, many people came away from an encounter with Dorothy absolutely convinced they were the *only* ones who knew and understood the "real" Parker. In fact, of course, she had simply been very adroit at confirming the egocentricity endemic to every eager conversationalist.

Enough Rope had made Dorothy a kind of national institution, America's poet laureate of sarcastic intuitions about love, life and the relations between the sexes. Her reputation was further enhanced by her regular "Constant Reader" book reviews in *The New Yorker*, which began appearing in 1927. Dorothy was as fearless and sardonic when taking on authors as she had been when, ten years earlier, she had reviewed plays for *Vanity Fair*. Her comments, for example, about Lady Margot Asquith's *Lay Sermons* are scalding. (Margot Asquith, 1864–1945, was a well-known wit and wife of Britain's Prime Minister.) "I think it must be pleasanter to be Margot Asquith than to be any other living human being. . . . Her perfect confidence in herself is a thing to which monuments should be erected; hers is a poise that ought to be on display at the British

Museum. The affair between Margot Asquith and Margot Asquith will live as one of the prettiest love stories in all literature." And in a parting shot in the same review, Parker concluded: "*Lay Sermons* is a naive and an annoying and an unimportant book. The author says, 'I am not sure that my alternate choice for the name of this modest work is altogether happy.' Happier I think it would have been if, instead of the word 'Sermon' she had selected the word 'Off.' "

But if Parker could demolish books in a few phrases, she could also be a generous critic. Her 1928 review of Isadora Duncan's posthumous *My Life* shows Dorothy at her sensitive best. She admits the book is badly written—"There are veritable Hampton Court mazes of sentences"—but still praises Duncan's autobiography as "enormously interesting and. . . . profoundly moving." "Please read Isadora Duncan's *My Life*," Dorothy concludes. "You will find you won't care how it is written; you will find you will not be able to trace to their sources the current rumors that it has been expurgated. There is enough in these pages. Here is the record of a grand person."

It may well be that Dorothy Parker empathized especially with Isadora Duncan, for there were certain parallels between them. Both had trying personalities and were driven compulsively to self-dramatizing gestures. Yet both were women of extraordinary talent and passion for living. When Parker described Duncan as a "magnificent, generous, gallant, reckless fated fool of a woman," she might well have been speaking of herself. But Parker, perhaps even more than Duncan, experienced a sense of entrapment in a world too small, too petty for the "magnificent" ones, and this feeling of captivity was in some part responsible for Parker's self-destructiveness. Diana Forbes-Robertson, Vincent Sheean's wife, observed that Dorothy drank "because of her perception. She wanted to dull her perceptions. Her vision of life was almost more than she could bear. . . . Did she suffer from the most overpowering ego? Did she wonder if everybody was stupid? Was she suffering from being so damned clever? . . . I wonder if that extremely apologetic way of hers wasn't a supreme effort to hide the contempt she may have felt. . . . Possibly she was a very amiable character. But what she was, was sheer charm that made you forget everything else."

Dorothy Parker made another observation about Isadora Duncan which could as well have applied to herself. About Isadora's lovers: "She had a knack for selecting the unworthy—perhaps all great women have." By this criterion, Parker was certainly great. Her friends were constantly amazed, and embarrassed, by Dorothy's choice of men; each one seemed more inferior than the last. A succession of Eddie-like lovers—handsome but uninteresting Wall Street types—came and went, most of them doing far more harm than good to Parker's life. In 1928 it was another businessman, John Garrett, but by the next year she had tired of him, and her personal life drifted along aimlessly, as the nation sped on toward the Crash. Her second collection of verse, *Sunset Gun*, had appeared in 1928, but Parker's writing career was still unfocused. Her editors and publishers grew increasingly exasperated at her tendency to avoid promised work, invent alibis and introduce massive alterations after her writing had already gone to page proofs.

George Oppenheimer, her editor at Viking (which

published her collection of short stories, *Laments for the Living*) recounts a characteristic incident. Dorothy was supposed to have been reading and correcting the page proofs for *Laments*, but had neglected them altogether. (She was, in truth, so dissatisfied with her work that she wanted to burn the proofs.) Taking the bull by the horns, Oppenheimer brought himself, the proofs and a bottle of whiskey to a friend's house, where Dorothy was staying. He locked himself, the whiskey and Dorothy in a quiet room. "The more she drank," Oppenheimer recalled, "the less she liked what she had written, but a few drinks more and she mellowed, and put the proofs into shape."

It was said and believed by many of her closest associates that Dorothy simply hated to write. That, if true at all, is only a partial explanation. Parker was a perfectionist, a trait common to many alcoholics. It either had to be perfect, or it absolutely couldn't be done at all. And, as exasperating as it often was to her editors, her habit of perfection paid off in her art. Parker's short stories, especially, reveal that much-envied architectonic quality: not one word out of place, not a single one which could be omitted without destroying the whole.

But however much, and for whatever reasons, Parker may have found writing difficult, it remained her calling; she continued to write professionally until her death in 1967. Nearly all of the work on which her reputation rests, however, was written in the twenties or early thirties. In fact, a particularly important aspect of her writings is the way in which they capture the atmosphere of the twenties, and the sense of "lostness" felt by many, the perception that the American dream had turned out to be hollow and shabby after all. Parker caught, too, the desperate ambiance of the jazz age, with its hectic rhythms and improvisational quality. When the twenties changed into the thirties, Dorothy Parker's most important "inspiration" as a writer slipped away too.

In 1930, Dorothy left for Europe, where she stayed for more than a year. The Manhattan scene was dead, and perhaps Dorothy wanted to skip the funeral.

Alexander Woollcott once remarked that Dorothy Parker was a rare combination of Lady Macbeth and Little Nell. She could cling to a person's arm (especially a man's), looking up softly and helplessly—and in the next moment stab her hapless companion in the back. This turnabout character caused Dorothy, and others, a good deal of unhappiness, but it also seems to have been part of her attractiveness. Dorothy Parker's ability to attract men (even, as she grew older, much younger men) was remarkable. She had an indefatigable—and very elegant—flirtatiousness which seems to have made men feel masculine, buoyant and talented. Yet some of the more thoughtful men who met her were disturbed by the extremeness of her seeming coquetry. Edmund Wilson wrote of his first meeting with Dorothy, just after World War I, that "she had been, I thought, overperfumed, and the hand with which I had shaken hers kept the scent of her perfume all day. Although she was fairly pretty, and although I needed a girl, what I considered the vulgarity of her too much perfume prevented me from paying her court."

Nevertheless, plenty of others were perfectly willing to be charmed by Dorothy, even though the effect was usually only temporary. When she returned from Europe in 1931, Parker moved straight into the Algonquin and started an affair with one John McClain, a young stockbroker and self-professed "he-whore," who made a point of proclaiming in detail his intimacies with Parker to whomever would listen. When the affair ran aground, McClain accusing Parker of possessiveness and she accusing him of neglect, the two staged a grand finale in which McClain bolted from Parker's room, shouting, "You're a lousy lay!" Dorothy calmly explained to a friend, "Yes, his body went to his head."

McClain may well have been the most abysmal of Parker's liaisons, and perhaps it was as a result of this experience that Parker began to look for a different kind of relationship. To the distinct surprise of most of her friends, in 1933 Parker married a young actor, Alan Campbell. Campbell met only one of Dorothy's proclaimed criteria—he was neither stupid nor ruthless, but he was extremely handsome. In fact, Alan Campbell was sweet-tempered and easy-going; he respected Dorothy and was genuinely devoted to her. Campbell's role in Dorothy Parker's life turned out to be not dissimilar to Eugen Boissevain's in Edna St. Vincent Millay's: he took her in charge, organized her life, took care of the housekeeping, paid the bills, monitored her drinking, and, most importantly, saw to it that she wrote.

Campbell himself was a capable writer, and soon became Dorothy's collaborator. After the couple honeymooned at George Oppenheimer's house in California, where Robert Benchley was already working as a Hollywood screenwriter, Campbell and Parker decided to move to the West Coast themselves, and Dorothy Parker's screenwriting career began, at a starting salary of $5,200 a week —a fortune in Depression terms. Campbell was her writing partner as well as her personal support system, and the two of them made a great deal of money, although Parker was never pleased with the work they did, or indeed with anything at all about Hollywood.

"Hollywood smells like a laundry," Dorothy told Ward Morehouse of *The New York World-Telegram*. "The beautiful vegetables taste as if they were raised in trunks. . . . Sure you make money writing on the coast, and God knows you earn it, but that money is like so much compressed snow. It goes so fast it melts in your hand." In spite of her lucrative success, Parker detested Hollywood, and left it whenever she could.

Parker's Hollywood years represented a kind of cul-de-sac; she was too individualistic to fit into the studio system and never adapted her creative writing for it. In his *New Yorker* review of the Viking *Portable Dorothy Parker*, Edmund Wilson complained that Dorothy made the mistake of not really getting her teeth into Hollywood as she was so well qualified to do. The sunshine Babylon did not inspire her best barbs and most cutting satire. Too, during her Hollywood years, like so many other American writers, she was sidetracked by leftist causes, which never dovetailed in any important way with her artistic intuitions.

As can easily be imagined, the Parker/Campbell marriage was a stormy one, and shortly after World War II they divorced. One of Parker's best friends, Donald

Ogden Stewart, expressed the opinion that Dorothy was really incapable of love:

> Dottie was attractive to everybody. . . . It wasn't difficult to fall in love with her. . . . But I think if you had been married to Dottie, you would have found out, little by little, that she really wasn't there. She was in love with you, let's say, but it was *her* emotion; she was not worrying about *your* emotion. You couldn't put your finger on her. If you ever married her, you would find out eventually. She was both wide open and the goddamndest fortress at the same time.

Still, Alan Campbell seems to have been the one man who could "take it." In 1950, after several years of divorce, Campbell and Parker remarried, remaining together until his death in 1963. All of Parker's problems continued—and worsened; she grew fat and puffy, and her drinking increased in spite of Campbell's efforts. Although she seems to have loved Campbell, she often turned on him, spilling out all her hatred in a torrent of words. But without Campbell's presence in her life, Dorothy Parker's last years might easily have been much worse. Even her most loyal friends found Dorothy's last decade difficult to endure. Lillian Hellman wrote that she found it painful to be around Parker toward the end of her life. "I found that Dottie's middle age, old age, made rock of much of what had been fluid and eccentricities once charming became too strange for safety or comfort."

That in spite of her drinking and her unassuageable sadness Parker continued writing is a tribute to the force of her talent. Although she took refuge in regarding herself as a "has-been" ("Let's face it, honey, my verse is terribly dated," she told an interviewer from *Paris Review* in 1957), Parker was nevertheless in some demand, and the encouragement to write—and get paid for it—was always there. Starting in the mid-fifties Dorothy Parker became a regular contributor to *Esquire* magazine, receiving $750 per month for her contributions. The alliance was an apt one, as *Esquire*'s founding publisher Arnold Gingrich must have perceived, and if she had been as productive as promised, Parker could have livened up that monthly, whose arch, devil-may-care quality fit Parker's style to a T. When Parker actually wrote the stuff she promised, everything worked out marvelously, but a great deal of the time after the mid-fifties she was ill, incapacitated, or simply unmotivated. The *Esquire* editors had to prod her constantly, and sometimes she would falsely claim that her monthly piece was in the mail, insisting that the editors must have lost it in the office. She went on collecting her monthly check, but turned in only half the promised material.

What she did write, however, never lost its punch or professional gloss. Even in the four years after Alan Campbell's death, when she lived alone and lonely in New York's Volney Hotel, Parker collaborated on a play with Arnaud d'Usseau, with whom she had worked in Hollywood. *Ladies of the Corridor* is about women living out their lives in the public isolation of a hotel very like the Volney, and the play is filled with some really delicious Parker wit, some of her best whiplash humor. It is also covered by a cloud of grim mortality. The women suffer from boredom and uselessness, and the sad awareness that their last hold on life is slipping away in a succession of wasted days.

"Do you know what they do when you die in this hotel?" Dorothy asked a young reporter who came to interview her at the Volney. "They used to take them down on the big elevator in the back, but it's not running, and they take them down that front elevator, and you know how small it is. They have to stand you up." This macabre irony was a vein which ran through all of Parker's work and life. Back in the Round Table days, she and Robert Benchley had subscribed to a number of publications from the undertaker's trade—partly as a joke, but partly to appease a hovering curiosity about the physical fact of death. This fascination with death often lay just below the surface of Parker's humor, as in her famous "Rhyme Against the Living" from *Sunset Gun*:

> If wild my breast and sore my pride,
> I bask in dreams of suicide;
> If cool my heart and high my head,
> I think, "How lucky are the dead!"

As always, the ironic swipe at herself, delivered so tartly that the reader winces—and yet revealing an almost pathetic vulnerability.

Parker's very great talent as a writer seems to have been rooted in a bone-tingling fear that the next step was into oblivion—that whatever she tried to grasp would pull back, melt, like Hollywood money. In a sense, her life was a sad and lonely story of personal disappointments, of reaching out and not finding. But in another sense, perhaps, it was a story of triumphant survival. Harold Hays, the young *Esquire* editor who was sent to talk to Parker when she was about sixty, recalled that he expected to find an old wisecracking hotshot, but was amazed to discover that Dorothy Parker was "a genuinely warm woman with a sense of great dignity, an old-fashioned great lady." And so she was, too. There was no falseness about it. A very real intelligence and sensitivity persisted under her well-defended persona, and that is what made her a writer of substance, not just a novelty.

Even her sharply funny two- and four-line verses deserve much more credit than they are usually given. While it may be true that Parker's originality as a writer is less evident in her poetry than in her stories, her contribution to American verse shouldn't be ignored. Henry Sidel Canby, reviewing her *Death and Taxes* (1931) in *The Saturday Review*, had the insight to recognize that what Parker was attempting in English poetry was the creation of a satirical verse comparable to that of the classical Latin poets. The technical precision of her lines reveals a poet who not only has imagination but a superbly disciplined mastery of her craft as well. "I suspect that one should quote Latin rather than English," Canby wrote, "to parallel the edged fineness of Dorothy Parker's verse. This belle dame sans merci has the ruthlessness of the great tragic lyricists whose work was allegorized in the fable of the nightingale singing with her breast against a thorn. It is disillusionment recollected in tranquility where the imagination has at last controlled the emotions. It comes out clear, and with the authentic sparkle of a great vintage."

Her stories were characterized by a similar precision, both in insight and execution. Parker created in her fiction brilliant and sardonic studies of urban life in the twenties. Her stories amplified the undertones of unhappiness which

lay beneath the glittering surface. Parker was able to create a portrait of this life because she lived it. The world she wrote about was the world she knew—the world of the city and of washed-out suburbia, of people shining with success and living well, but whose inner life had been snuffed out, victims of the airlessness and purposelessness of modern life, of getting and spending, of conspicuous consumption. Dorothy Parker's world was that of the banal cocktail party, of the housewife's coffee klatsch, of women trying to make it on their own, and failing, or succeeding to no avail; her stories chronicle the aimless and insensate love affairs of the traveling salesman or Wall Street broker, the world of the summer hotel, the weekend that doesn't refresh, the whiskey that no longer works.

Dorothy Parker could write so poignantly and so truthfully about a character like Hazel Morse, the "Big Blonde," because she herself stood always poised at the edge of the same quicksand; she knew the territory and wrote about it with uncommon quality and originality. As Edmund Wilson observed, Parker had a value derived from rarity—a "rarity like that of steel penknives, good erasers and real canned sardines, articles of which the supply has almost given out, and of which one is only now beginning to be aware of how excellent the quality was." Although she was always "kidding around," her witticisms were drenched in bitter and tragic irony; her writings capture the dark, gloomy substratum of twentieth century life as perfectly as they do the snappy, bubbling surface.

Parker's best stories can be read today without so much as a footnote—so accurate are they at the level of deep truth about human beings, their motives, masks and madnesses. And always she accomplished this not through the epic tale of sweeping vision, but much more originally, through the small focus on the experience of everyday life: the "slice-of-life" story, that series of precisely observed details which, without any editorializing by the author, sharply defines a truth; and the "soliloquy," Parker's own invention to turn the feminine experience inside out. The ordinary, seemingly superficial world Parker depicts is teeming with the hopes and fears we all recognize as the compelling stuff of life.

"It's not the tragedies that kill us," Dorothy Parker observed in the *Paris Review* interview, "it's the messes. I can't stand messes. I'm not being a smart cracker. You know I'm not when you meet me—don't you, honey?"

8

ANITA LOOS

Anita Loos was not exactly a child in pigtails (as she sometimes suggested) when she became a screenwriter. But she *was* less than twenty, a petite four feet eleven inches, and still playing Little Lord Fauntleroy when she saw a short silent film and immediately decided to write one better.

But how to get started with these little celluloid confections? Where could she send a script? The next morning, before rehearsal, Anita climbed up into the projection booth to search for a film can that might have an address to which she could send a story. The address she found was: The American Biograph Company, 11 East Fourteenth Street, New York, New York. In a single morning of free time Anita dashed off a screenplay called "The New York Hat," which she immediately shipped off to the Biograph Company. In a mere two weeks she had her answer in an impressive-looking envelope:

Mr. A Loos,
Dear Sir,
We have accepted your scenario entitled "The New York Hat." We enclose an assignment which kindly sign and have witnessed by two persons and then return. On receipt of signed assignment we shall send you our check for $25 in payment.
Yours very truly,
Thomas A. Dougherty

She didn't know it at the time, but Anita Loos had arrived in the movies at the very top—although the distance from top to bottom was not great in those days. Dougherty was the story editor for D. W. Griffith, the cinematic genius who innovated cross-cutting, close-ups, long shots and flashbacks in films. "The New York Hat" was indeed filmed, starring Lionel Barrymore, Lillian and Dorothy Gish, and Mary Pickford. The movie was something of a hit too.

The New York Hat was released in 1913. Sixty-eight years later, Loos was an energetic octogenarian, helping to put together for Grand Central Galleries in New York a show called "Anita Loos and Friends," documenting her friendships in the literary and entertainment worlds, from Douglas Fairbanks to H. G. Wells. Behind her lay a career that included over two hundred screenplays, the smash-hit book *Gentlemen Prefer Blondes*, a series of charming and thoughtful autobiographical works, and an almost legendary social life.

Through it all, Loos maintained an irreverent, comic/serious focus on sex in America, and her observations were as insightful as they were amusing. H. L. Mencken, after reading *Gentlemen Prefer Blondes*, inquired of Anita,

"Do you realize that you've made fun of sex, which has never before been done in this grand and glorious nation of ours?" Loos always took it to be an obvious truth that there was no bedrock of reality in the relationship between the sexes, that all was sport, that those who saw themselves as winning were the most obvious and hilarious losers, pinned down to victories that weren't worth the effort.

Because of her freewheeling and essentially comic attitude toward the relationship between the sexes—as in those one-reel farces of the early silent films—we are hardly inclined to think of Loos as a serious moralist or student of American mores. But although Loos was never a philosopher or a systematic thinker, she always forced her audience to think. She created fictional characters—like the archetypal "dumb blonde" Lorelei Lee—which seize and reveal some aspect of the American experience, showing it to be all at once hilarious, pathetic and a little scary. And in her numerous autobiographical sallies, Loos's powers of observation and analysis show us the poignant funniness of the perpetual soap opera called "everyday life." Although she certainly didn't set out to do any such thing, Anita Loos created a comic chronicle of that central American preoccupation, sex (or, as it is sometimes called, money).

In looking back on her own life, Anita Loos was never fully able to account for herself in terms of family background, at least not sufficiently to explain her alleged variance from the norm of American womanhood. She came, she said, "from a typically American hodge-podge of misfits, tossed together in a pioneer world that wasn't cramped by competition. But along with the razzle-dazzle supplied by its offbeat characters, there were certain elements of respectability." This combination of the colorful and the conventional was exemplified by her maternal grandmother, Cleopatra Fairbrother, who was bred in Shaker Village in Vermont, and avidly courted by a handsome Englishman named George Smith who had made a small fortune in the California Gold Rush of 1849. Endowed with a feverish wanderlust, Cleopatra immediately urged her new husband back to California, and hoped-for danger and excitement. Their family eventually included five children, among them Anita's docile, supernormal mother Minnie. Unaccountably, Minnie fell in love with the dashing Midwesterner and dedicated philanderer, R. Beers Loos.

The marriage of the flamboyant Beers Loos and the unflappable Minnie Smith was apparently a successful one in spite of Beers's womanizing. Anita grew up with a certain respect for her mother's absolute devotion and superb ability to keep her fragile marriage from shattering. Still, the young Anita was suspicious of the idea that women should sacrifice their own lives and careers for their husbands, and she came to have little patience with women who see their destinies as entirely tied up with the ability to get or hold a man. It was her father's freewheeling, devil-may-care spirit that she really admired. This is not to say that Anita would have preferred being a male. Rather, she saw the condition of being a woman in terms of a "game," something you "play" at being or doing, something wildly amusing and fanciful in its own right.

Obviously Anita was pretty. And knew it. No less a person than D. W. Griffith was derailed by this hoyden, for all he could think about on their first meeting was a way to turn Anita into another Mary Pickford, Mae Marsh or Mabel Normand. "Forget about screenwriting and become an actress," he pleaded. "That's what every little girl wants to do, isn't it?" But Anita didn't think of herself as just another pretty girl. She had come to the conclusion that visual appearance was not identical with inner self—a truth that she would spend most of her life attempting to make clear to the men who crossed her path. True, she wanted romance, excitement, glamour, but she soon found that she didn't want the variety of those things that appealed to the typical female in Hollywood. She liked the *role* of innocent and beguiling female, and she could with ease have allowed herself to be fished out of some icy river by strong masculine arms in the best tradition of Griffith's film beauties. But, Anita never saw her own *self* as one of these standardized heroines. Throughout her life, she regarded herself as a woman quite out of step with "things as they are" and as film makers want them to be.

Always aware of her little girl charm, but never really believing in its reality, she saw the feminine game as one which you play for the sheer curiosity of it, not with any ulterior motive. You bag a man like you trap some wild animal, not for any utilitarian purpose, not to secure domesticity, not to find social respectability, but *for the fun of it*, whatever that may be—for some yet further opportunity to see the world in an antic light, to get the circus moving. The battle of the sexes, Anita felt, was endless and pointless, but it made an amusing game.

The game began for Anita when she found herself, at a young age, a professional screenwriter. Like many another button-cute girl, Anita had attracted her share of boyfriends. But she was shocked to find that most of them turned away from her when they found out she wrote screenplays for a living. One early beau refused to believe that she was making any money writing for the movies. Of course it was all too easy to prove and, Anita wrote later, this caused an even more unfortunate reaction: "My beau didn't want to believe I was an authoress; it turned me into some kind of a monster; I no longer seemed to be a girl."

It didn't take Anita long to figure out that she was going to have trouble with men, and she tried to calculate what kind of man she might be able to capture who wouldn't run away from a young authoress. But she didn't do it the right way. In looking for the best path to take, she separated the men from the boys and then deliberately chose a boy—"a straw husband"—whom she thought she could dominate. Her miscalculation led to the first of two disastrous marriages.

The lad in question was named Frankie (or was it Freddy— Anita couldn't even remember herself after a few years). Young, innocent, Frankie (Freddy?) was the kind who would question nothing, not even a wife in show business. As the wedding day approached, though, Anita started to get cold feet and looked for a way out. Her mother pleaded with her; the guests were all invited, the flowers ordered, and so on. So the wedding took place, the vows were exchanged, the wedding night passed, Loos all the while convinced, as if from a progression of seemingly greater and more intense soakings of cold water, that married

life to this stripling simply could not be. On the morning after her wedding night, she was determined to flee, and sent her docile, uxorious bridegroom on a wild goose chase for some hard-to-get hairpins while she cleared out of their honeymoon bungalow. Her idea was to run immediately to D. W. Griffith and claim her due as a scriptwriter, and this is precisely what she did.

Not entirely without regret, as it turned out, for later on Anita ruefully admitted that she may have picked the right man—he had agreeably gone after the hairpins and was searching all over California to give them to her. But at a very inconvenient moment, Anita had simply decided something it often takes women years to discover, even today: that she wanted her independence more than she wanted a husband.

On some level, Anita herself probably recognized even then that any long-term relationship between herself and a man could only result in disaster for both. Her long marriage to screenwriter and director John Emerson was in fact to be just as chaotic in its own way as her day-long matrimonial escapade with poor young Freddy (or was it Frankie?). Perhaps this is why Anita developed a great respect for asexual relationships between men and women, and filled her life with close, valuable male friends. "May I here suggest," she wrote in *A Girl Like I*, "that Platonic friendship can definitely hold its own against the sex urge, that it is more enduring and, in my case, has provided several associations that ended only when their heroes died."

"Platonic" was the term Anita Loos preferred to describe her relationship with poet Vachel Lindsay in the early 1920s. At that time, she was already married to John

Emerson (though, like Amelia Earhart, Anita never regarded marriage as an institution requiring any medieval code of fidelity). Lindsay was one of the first "important" American writers to begin taking films seriously; prior to this time, even trade journals like *Variety* tended to ignore the movies or relegate their reviews to the back pages. But Vachel Lindsay had begun eulogizing silent films in such respectable literary magazines as the *Atlantic Monthly* and the *New Republic*. And it was while writing articles for these journals that Lindsay began complimenting in print Anita Loos's ability as a screenwriter.

Loos was so flattered by the poet's attention that she bought a book of his poems and, delighted by what she read, sent him a fan letter in care of his publisher. To her astonishment, Lindsay replied: "Be sure I have watched all your work with great interest and I keep you well in mind." That was the beginning of a warm correspondence between Loos and Lindsay which continued until the latter's suicide in 1931. Like all of Anita's relationships, the one with Lindsay was to have a component of comic melodrama, which became apparent in an early funny/sad episode. Lindsay was so struck by Mae Marsh's performance in *The Wild Girl* that he was moved to write this poem:

> She is Madonna in an art
> As wild and young as her sweet eyes,
> A frail dew flower from this hot lamp
> That is today's divine surprise.

Marsh, who considered herself "an intellectual gink," begged her friend Anita to act as a ghostwriter, so she could send Lindsay a reply worthy of his literary attention. "I thus

developed," Loos recalled, "into a small female Cyrano de Bergerac, sending the poet some much more emotional thoughts on life and love than I ventured in my own purely intellectual correspondence with him. Mae copied my innermost thoughts in her own handwriting, and Vachel's replies became increasingly ardent. In no time at all he was falling madly in love with Mae."

Initially, Anita later confided to friends, she was jealous of Mae's success with Lindsay—a success which, after all, her own skill at writing had helped bring about. Then it turned out that all three parties in this ménage were actually to meet in New York. Mae and Anita were traveling there on film business, while Lindsay was to be there for a poetry reading. (A train ride from California to New York was itself an adventure in the twenties, and the two women were hoping for some romantic diversion to help pass the time. Unfortunately, they were not even so much as flirted with. Anita wryly commented, "Western men seem to lack not only gallantry but even interest. It is rather revealing that in all the Western movies cowboys seem to caress only their ponies.")

Upon arriving in New York, Anita and Mae checked in at a suite in the Algonquin Hotel, in part because Loos had heard of the Round Table and knew its members regularly had lunch there. Very shortly, though, Loos and Marsh moved into an apartment, since D. W. Griffith, whose film *Intolerance* the two were in New York to promote (Anita had written the screenplay; Mae had starred in it), had decided to stay on the East Coast for a season to do some outdoor filming. Anita, who had never even been outside her native state of California, began to feel like a "bona fide New Yorker." Soon, Vachel Lindsay appeared in New York in the flesh and made an appointment to meet Mae and Anita for tea at their apartment. The stage was set for seduction. Anita's mother, who was staying with them in New York, had been shipped off to New Jersey to visit an aunt. Anita herself planned to be present only until the ice was broken, after which she would disappear "to do some work." The apartment had been arranged for "atmosphere":

> Before teatime [Loos wrote in *A Girl Like I*] Mae and I spent hours on a decor that featured a number of heavy cut-glass vases which we had filled with long stemmed American Beauty roses. We softened the light effect by putting pink bulbs in all the lamps, and the air was perfumed with incense especially imported from Chinatown. Mae's freckles had disappeared under a coat of make-up, and as a gown worthy of the occasion she chose a green and gold Fortuny robe of the crinkled type which clung to her slim figure and even trailed a little bit. With her red-gold hair drifting in waves to her shoulders, Mae moved through the rosy atmosphere like Melisande.

In the event, however, Mae was so flustered by Lindsay's "cornfield" appearance and manner that she fled, leaving Anita with Vachel on her hands. Anita, who viewed all such situations as part of the "game" that rules the relations between the sexes, coped with the whole business quite well, and spent much of the next two weeks exploring New York with Lindsay, until he was forced to return to his home in Springfield, Illinois. Many years later Anita remarked that the poet's "roaring bumptiousness was the camouflage of a tremendously sad man. Anyone as sensitive

to physical beauty as he must have flinched at the sight of every mirror. Certainly he was lonely and avid for companionship; at any rate, he clutched at mine."

In later years Lindsay wanted Loos to marry him, but then Vachel never ceased falling in love with *someone* —"as a poet should," Anita observed. He would write Loos about his crushes, but sadly, his search for "the pioneer maiden with whom he could live out his own version of the American dream" (in Anita's description) remained elusive and unfulfilled. In one of his last letters, Vachel wrote Anita:

> "He who lives more lives than one, more deaths than one must die."
>
> I hope you will think of me just as a person—unofficially as it were, once in a while. You have your picture on my wall so I see you every day.

Lindsay's tragic suicide symbolized to Anita "the failure of the American dream to live up to its rugged past." This failure was not, she felt, merely the inability of an occasional individual to find success in a chosen vocation; the trouble was deeper, more malignant, and one of its symptoms was the estrangement of the sexes.

The friendship between Anita Loos and Vachel Lindsay was characteristic of many which unfolded against the background of her strange and unfulfilling marriage to John Emerson, which began in 1919 and never exactly ended. Superficially, Loos and Emerson had a great deal in common, at least to begin with. Both were screenwriters, and both saw Hollywood social life in comic terms. But Emerson soon discovered, to his chagrin, that his wife had more talent than he did; rather than admit it, he suggested giving up Hollywood for a life of leisure. Thus he would be sure that his wife didn't make any more money than he did. He had no objections to his wife's career as a screenwriter as long as it was subordinate to his own, a kind of hobby or vocation, but when it loomed too large and threatened to overshadow his own reputation, he was deeply threatened. The couple did leave Hollywood for New York, where they lived out the affluent twenties—sometimes together, sometimes separately. With the coming of the Depression in the early thirties, however, Emerson was forced to permit Anita to go back to Hollywood to restore their severely eroded family fortune, and the effects of this were shattering and irreversible.

Loos's autobiographies chronicle all sorts of mayhem that Emerson let loose in the marital arena—hypochondriacal episodes, homicidal threats, and of course, chorus girls. From the very beginning, Emerson insisted that he and Anita spend every Tuesday evening apart, doing whatever they wished, with no questions asked. Anita hated the idea at first, but after a while it ceased to make any difference. She eventually found out that John Emerson "rather pathetically . . . used to take his dates to the same plays we had seen together and would entertain them, second-hand, with cracks I had made. . . . " Sometimes he would even ask Anita to read other women's love letters to him aloud.

Emerson also had what Loos called "astonishing

caprices." On one occasion, for example, Emerson had returned home late from a committee meeting for Actors Equity (he was heavily involved in the campaign for actors' rights) but found he was too keyed up to sleep. His insomnia that night was further complicated by the smell of laundry soap on the bed sheets, a defect that could be remedied, John assured Anita, *only* by sprinkling them with violet cologne. Since it was then three in the morning and all the shops were closed, securing the cologne required enormous improvisatory skills. Undaunted, Anita learned from a telephone operator of an all-night drugstore at Grand Central Station. "It was a long way to 42nd Street," Anita recalled, "but it intrigued me no end to cover my dishabille with a trench coat, pull a slouch hat over my eyes, and start out into the night, a lone female on a strange mission." Reaching the drugstore at last, Anita made her purchase and hurried home with the foolproof remedy for insomnia. When she got to the bedroom she found John sound asleep. "He slept until morning and never mentioned violet cologne again."

Her experiences with Emerson led Loos to reflect on the fate of the male in contemporary society. In a chapter of *Kiss Hollywood Good-by* called "Once Again the Caveman," she wrote:

> Mr. E. [John Emerson] was actually the forerunner of a type that was beginning to emerge in our country. From early colonial days, sex life in America had been based on the custom of men supporting women. That situation reached its heyday in the Twenties when it was easy for any dabbler in stocks to flaunt his manhood by lavishing an unearned income on girls. But with the stock market crash, men were hard

> put even to keep their wives, let alone spend money on sex outside the home. The adjustment was much easier on women than on men, who jumped out of windows in droves, whereas I can't recall a single headline that read: KEPT GIRL LEAPS FROM LOVE NEST.

Sex and money—or sex as money—had become Anita's theme early on, and remained the focus of her wry observations of American life. In her most famous, successful, and irresistibly funny book, *Gentlemen Prefer Blondes*, Loos popularized and identified for the first time that category of feminine existence called "the dumb blonde." Loos was fond of reporting that the idea for writing *Gentlemen Prefer Blondes* popped into her head during a train trip. A group of what Anita termed "the Hollywood elite" (that is, those who were never really fond of Hollywood) were returning from New York on the Santa Fe *Chief*. Among the assembled company was a gorgeous blonde who was being imported to Hollywood to be the leading lady in Douglas Fairbanks's next film. Now this young woman was hale, hearty, and hefty, literally towering over the tiny Anita, but she was "waited on, catered to and cajoled" by the entire male company, while poor, diminutive Anita was allowed to lug heavy suitcases and hoist them up to their racks while the men stood around, completely indifferent.

Obviously, Anita later reflected, there was some important difference between herself and that blonde. Both were young, both attractive. Could the difference be blondeness itself? Thinking over all the blondes she knew—including a number who had been recruited for Hollywood from the Ziegfeld Follies—Anita's mind drifted to the dumbest blonde she knew, a girl who had bewitched

even the great sage of Baltimore, H. L. Mencken. Here was a man of the keenest intelligence and wit, a man who included Anita in his close circle of friends, a man to whom a cerebral appeal ought to have meant everything. Yet when it came down to the clinch, when it came to picking a female who moved him off his chair, Mencken picked a witless blonde.

The whole thing was completely unjust, thought Anita. Seated in her compartment as the train raced across the plains of Kansas, Anita reached for one of the large yellow pads on which she created movie scenarios, and in a rage of comic abandon began the composition of *Gentlemen Prefer Blondes*. At first it was to be nothing more than a magazine story, and in a moment of pique and female guile she sent it to Mencken, who was about to begin his sophisticated monthly, *The American Mercury*. Mencken was tickled by the story, but didn't think it would quite fit in at the *Mercury*; he advised Anita to send the story to *Harper's Bazaar*, "where it will get lost among the ads and won't offend anybody." This Anita did, and so delighted was editor Henry Sell with the story that he urged Anita to go on with further installments. These ran in serial form and were soon eagerly awaited around the country—making Anita, then an obscure and half-retired screenwriter, a figure of national note. The series also made Lorelei Lee an American institution.

The plot of *Gentlemen* was simplicity itself—mere froth. Lorelei Lee, a dumb blonde adventurer from Little Rock, Arkansas (Mencken's idea of the American capital of stupidity and banality), attaches herself to Gus Eisman of Chicago (Gus Eisman, "the button King,"), and takes that gentleman for the ride of his life, always with addlepated charm and guile. At Mr. Eisman's expense, Lorelei and a girlfriend travel around Europe, which continent provides an excellent showcase for their purely American inanity and vacuity, and an excellent waste receptacle for poor Eisman's hard-earned dollars. The thesis, of course, is that if you are blonde, and if you can exhibit the most rudimentary and simple-minded form of sex appeal, you can easily make your way in a society given over to getting and spending, but seldom to thinking.

The collected installments of *Gentlemen* appeared in book form in November of 1926. The first printing was only twelve hundred copies, and by noon of the day it appeared, the entire edition was sold out. Loos's publishers immediately ordered a whopping second printing of 65,000 copies, and Anita's career as a bestselling author was launched—not with a whimper but with a bang. Many readers of the book did not, of course, pay much attention to its underlying message, and thus missed the fact that *Gentlemen Prefer Blondes* is not only a funny book, it is also a broadside aimed at American life.

The words "blonde" and "gentlemen" were both used ironically in Loos's title. How much of a gentleman, after all, can a "Button King" be? And a "blonde" is not merely someone born with light-colored hair; being a blonde is a state of mind. Any woman can be a blonde, even without the help of peroxide, simply by being willing to sail through life as a sexual appendage or ornament. In *Gentlemen*, Loos was lampooning mindless sexuality, but even more seriously, she was describing the decline of culture and the estrangement of the sexes. Loos believed that

in our society men have become "slender reeds," (drained, perhaps, by the American commercial ethic) who use women mainly to bolster their egos. This combination of ego-depleted males and "blondes" like Lorelei Lee, who can never rise above feeding the male ego a very meager diet, could only result, Loos thought, in an essential weakening of our civilization.

Loos contemplated the blonde question more somberly in a chapter of *Kiss Hollywood Good-by* called "What Killed Jean Harlow?" Harlow, Hollywood's platinum "Blonde Bombshell" (the title of a film of hers released in 1933), died of apparent alcohol and drug overdoses in 1937. But the clinical "cause of death" missed the point, in Anita's view. Jean Harlow died because "she had refused to put up a fight"—because, Loos insisted, she lacked the egomania necessary in an actress. Always lonely, Harlow longed for companionship in a lover, but her very looks stood in the way; she became, in Loos's phrase, "nothing more than a booby trap for male stupidity," the sort of woman who inevitably attracts "the dull type of gentlemen who prefer blondes."

Harlow's second husband, the quiet and self-effacing Paul Bern, was impotent—a "German psycho," Anita called him. Why Harlow chose to marry him is mystifying, except that she was desperate to get away from the house where her mother's husband, Marino Bello, was forever trying to seduce her. Bern apparently tried to deal with his impotence "by practices which Jean was too normal to accept." Tolerantly, she told Bern (according to Loos's account) to "find someone" for these sex sessions. "I won't object; I'll understand," she promised him. Bern responded to her tolerance by committing suicide. Harlow found him sprawled on his bedroom floor, naked, with a bullet hole in his head. "Paul Bern's suicide," Loos reflected, "was the very apotheosis of masochism, for he had killed himself while looking in a full-length mirror."

For Loos, this tragedy dramatized what happens when a man and a woman who both have small egos come together. The key to restoring balance in the relation between the sexes will not be found, Anita believed, in ego-deflation on either side. Women's liberation will not achieve its goal by diminishing the male ego still further. It has already been diminished, Loos contended, virtually to the point of extinction. Paul Bern's impotence was a physical emblem of the modern male's self-doubt, his feeling of increasing uselessness in every significant area of life —companionship, sex, work, money, recreation.

Through all of Anita Loos's writing about men there runs a vein of sadness, even pity. Much of this feeling must have come from her marriage to John Emerson, which, she wrote, was to her a bore, but to Emerson "a tragedy." The other men she knew, however, also seemed to evoke as much sympathy as affection. H. L. Mencken, whose friendship was an important part of Anita's life, was a good example. Mencken was the editor of fashionable magazines like the *Smart Set*, and his scathing critiques of American life were a much talked-about feature of the *Baltimore Sun*. Yet Mencken himself was a homebody who cared lovingly for his aging mother and gave Saturday night beer parties for his male friends. Anita spent many evenings at Luchow's (which Mencken frequented because, during prohibition, Luchow's provided "genuine

Würzburger beer disguised in teacups") listening to H. L. and his friends attacking virtually everything, and especially American religion. But, Anita came to realize, Mencken himself was a rather religious man, vulnerable to the very emotions he struggled to deny. He was, moreover, "a man of honor in the most old-fashioned sense," and suffered real distress over the declining quality of American taste and character.

Sherwood Anderson was in many ways the antithesis of H. L. Mencken: Mencken, boyish and blue-eyed, Anderson "monumental, big-boned, rugged," with "a shock of graying hair that served to accent his leonine appearance." Mencken hated New York, with what he called its "glittering swinishness"; Anderson loved it. Yet Anita was just as close to Anderson as to Mencken, and seems to have found him just as touching. Anderson's "masochistic career of divorcing and marrying one woman after another" was, from Anita's point of view, another evidence of the painful breach between the sexes.

Men, Anita believed, were turning more and more to a world of their own, a masculine world of sports, politics, and commerce; they were a little in love with their candidates and heroes, mistrustful of their own feelings for women. (After all, mused Anita, hadn't some doctor in Vienna proved that all sexual feelings were neurotic?) Women, for their part, withdrew into a feminine realm, like the one in which Anita participated in the stylish New York of the twenties. She and the "girls" had a round-robin of parties, sometimes held at Anita's, sometimes at the Talmadge sisters' suite at the Ambassador Hotel or at chorus-girl Marion Davies's brownstone on Riverside Drive. "Our parties, while exceedingly gay, were enlivened only by youthful high spirits, giggling, gossip, soft drinks, or, at most, the type of sweet concoctions that are mildly flavored with gin," Anita wrote in *A Girl Like I*. "We cherished an escape from the coquetry required when men were around, while the opportunity to take those same men apart and catalogue their faults was very refreshing."

By her own account, Loos viewed her affairs and marriages—as well as those of others—as a comic soap opera. This idea came to her early, when she found herself a reluctant and somewhat baffled participant in a complex triangle. During her "courtship" with John Emerson, Anita met Emerson's old friend Rayne Adams. Adams was a handsome architect in his late thirties, with dark, slightly graying hair. With his medium build and rather professional looks, he resembled John Emerson. "But there," Anita was later to write, "the resemblance ceased. While he was a gentle misanthrope and no smart aleck, Rayne had a healthy disrespect for all things that impressed John Emerson."

All the same, the two men were unusually closely linked. After Emerson's first wife had divorced him, she had married Adams. These three had then become close companions, "one of those involved situations which develop in worldly circles," Anita dryly observed. When Adams's wife (Emerson's first) died a year after their marriage, Rayne and John grew even closer together.

Perhaps it was not surprising, then, that when Anita Loos entered Emerson's life she entered, willy-nilly, Rayne's as well. During a long postoperative convalescence

in the hospital prior to his marrying Anita, John was visited by Rayne every day. Anita didn't find this particularly unusual until Adams told her his real reason for such solicitude: "I come here on account of you." Then, while Anita and Rayne were walking outside the hospital one evening, he gestured toward a light in one window and said:

> "Do you see that light? It was in that room that my wife died. . . . And because she died, I can ask the one girl I ever loved to marry me."

For once Anita was aphasic. She couldn't believe Adams was serious—or sane either, for that matter. "The proposal seemed so fantastic," she remembered years later, "I still couldn't believe that Rayne meant me; he finally had to tell me so in that three-word statement which is our main reward for living. The situation packed more punch than any I had ever dared to write: the widower of John's ex-wife now wanted to marry John's sweetheart. It gave a girl a very healthy respect for soap opera, which I have never lost."

Anita turned down Rayne's proposal, in large part because he was *too* devoted to her "and required nothing in return." She couldn't stand the thought of marrying someone whose love took the undiscriminating form of pet-like adoration and loyalty. Loos needed someone she could fight with, struggle against.

Nevertheless, over the years she did keep up an affectionate relationship with Rayne Adams. Their letters were tender and teasing. Once, after Loos and Emerson had had a big row, Adams wrote her from Paris:

> Anita dear,
> . . . you write concerning an altercation with John—but if it eases you at all, you are free to consider yourself married to me. It doesn't do any harm and you can have the thrills, anytime you wish, that come with infidelity.

And in another amusing note from Paris on the eve of her wedding to Emerson, Adams told Anita:

> I am sending you a suitable wedding gift, a book with a chapter devoted to "Jesus in the Bridal Chamber." In the opinion of this writer, most brides do not enter that chamber with their thoughts fixed sufficiently on Jesus. But I am also sending you a much better gift, which is my wish that you and John may be happy forever and ever.

Anita was one of those rare individuals capable of keeping affection for—and from—those with whom she had once been, in one way or another, romantically linked. But marriage, especially marriage to John Emerson, was another matter. Looking back on their relationship several decades later, Loos accused herself of being, as a young bride, too eager to please her husband—a fallacy Anita came to believe was characteristic of "blondes." (Loos was herself a brunette, but she could, by her own admission, occasionally fall into blonde behaviors.) The result was years of catering to Emerson's whims, enduring his affairs, and tolerating his condescension. When Anita would discover a bill for a present to one of his girlfriends, Emerson would explain cheerfully, "You're so generous, Buggie [Anita's nickname], that I have to be with some gold-digger from time to time in order to appreciate you."

The day finally arrived when she found a letter from one of John's fellow socialists, a woman who expressed her joy over "being able to compensate for his unfulfilled marriage." Confronted with this evidence, John did what many American men do in similar situations: he broke down and cried. Disarmed by having made a grown man weep, Anita asked Emerson if he wanted a divorce. "No, no, no, Buggie! I'll never leave you; you're so gullible you might fall into the hands of some crook who'd get hold of your money." Since Emerson had used up a good deal of Anita's money himself, this comment seemed particularly surreal.

They worked out a "solution." John found Anita an apartment on East Seventy-ninth Street and provided her with an "allowance," while he moved into bachelor quarters twenty blocks away. It was over—sort of.

The "war" between the sexes, in Anita's view, was really a stand-off, a kind of cold war in which espionage was more important than open combat. She herself was a spy—observing, analyzing, reporting. Even her youthful screenplays were comic peeps at the game-playing that goes on between men and women. A case in point is Anita's 1913 scenario "A Girl Like Mother." The story was about a young woman named Maude who is in love with Sidney, a stuffy youth who has sworn that he will never marry until he meets "a girl like Mother." Maude decides to resolve this situation by spying on Mom and finding out what is so special about her. Unfortunately she has gotten the wrong steer and believes the town trollop to be Sidney's mother. Although it goes completely against her nature to act in such a degrading manner, Maude begins to take on the mannerisms of the scarlet woman, shocking Sidney insensible. All ends well, however, since Maude manages to explain her odd behavior as the desperation of real love, and convinces Sidney that she is, in reality, "A Girl Like Mother."

Fifty years later, Loos was still musing on the subject of sex and sex appeal in *A Girl Like I*. Looking back on the twenties from the vantage point of the sixties, Anita had to say that, by comparison, sex in the twenties was pretty tame. "How could any epoch boast of passion with its hit love song bearing the title 'When You Wore a Tulip, a Bright Yellow Tulip, and I Wore a Big Red Rose'?" she inquires tartly. But all the same, the twenties as Loos lived them had an "audaciously romantic flavor." The game of sex was played with real sporting vigor, and yet was still touched by a child-like naivete.

Madame Frances—"sexy godmother to any number of Cinderellas"—provides a good example of the way romantic life in the twenties combined the fairy tale and the stock exchange. "The most prominent kept girls in New York" bought their clothes from Madame Frances in an elegant old whitestone residence in the East Fifties. The Madame herself, according to Loos, "was no beauty; her reddish hair was too frizzled, her blue eyes too sharp, and her figure too sturdy, but, as is so often the case, her romantic successes were even more spectacular than those of her beautiful clients. She had one quality which, as an attraction to men, far surpasses beauty: a robust love of life."

Madame Frances not only catered to girls whose sex appeal had already been discovered, she also cultivated the romantic potential of players who hadn't entered the game yet.

> She could spot undiscovered talent as expertly as did Flo Ziegfeld, and when her antenna picked up a girl of humble circumstances who was worthy to wear her dresses, Madame Frances would stake the girl to them, send her out into the nightspots with an escort, and then present the accumulated bills to the first rich admirer the girl attracted. The system didn't seem the least bit gross; in those days money was undefiled by taxes and so alluring that it brought out feelings of romance in girls. Had they ever left their love nests to wander with their keepers in Central Park, there would still be scores of trees bearing on their bark the tender legend "Baby Loves Daddy."

The wry sweetness Loos found in the sex/money connection was also to be glimpsed in other areas of life in the twenties. Although Anita did much of her "spying" in places like Madame Frances's, she also did a little reconnaissance wherever there seemed to be something interesting going on. One of her delights in the twenties was Harlem, where despite the congestion and dinginess, "every block was a pleasure zone and Lenox Avenue was a permanent carnival."

> Nobody wanted to stay indoors; tenants spilled over into the streets, where jazz was in the air; new rhythms were being extemporized that were giving America its first serious standing in the world of music. At Small's Paradise and the Savoy Ballroom the Charleston and Black Bottom were danced not as we did them, with a main thought toward showing

> off; the strut of Harlem was expressing an apotheosis of the human body that even our own high priestess of the dance, Isadora Duncan, admitted she could never achieve.

Racial prejudice was still blatant in the twenties, of course. Some blacks were able to "pass" in the white world of business by acquiring phony addresses and telephone numbers outside of Harlem, but most rejected this strategy, in part because they found the white community's love of business and finance unutterably boring. The values of blacks in Harlem were instinctively "more elegant than ours," Anita later recalled. And while most of the blacks she knew were tolerant of white people's mores, they had no desire to share them.

Perhaps this is part of the reason Anita was attracted to Harlem; she herself was tolerant of the human comedies which unfolded around her, but she preferred being an observer to being a participant. Although Lorelei Lee was conceived as "a symbol of the lowest possible mentality in our nation," nevertheless one cannot help but have a sneaking feeling that Lorelei and Anita are two versions of the same girl. Lorelei produces in the reader hilarious insights —entirely by reporting plausible events from her own whacky point of view. Anita Loos did exactly the same thing, just a bit more subtly.

"I have to begin to realize that I am one of the kind of girls that things happen to," mused Lorelei, and behind her voice we hear that of her creator. Anita Loos was at the center of things, from coast to coast, for the better part of a century—watching, listening, and laughing (a little sadly) all the way.

NOTES

The notes following provide references to works quoted or alluded to in the text of *Women of the Twenties,* as well as suggesting sources of further information.

Two sources which are cited frequently throughout the book are:

The Portable Dorothy Parker. Revised and enlarged edition, with a new introduction by Brendan Gill. New York: The Viking Press, 1974; paperback, Penguin Books, 1976. Copyright © 1973 by the National Association for the Advancement of Colored People. Introduction copyright © 1973 by Brendan Gill. Quotations from this work are reprinted by permission of The Viking Press.

Edmund Wilson, *The Twenties.* New York: Farrar, Straus and Giroux, 1975. Copyright © 1975 by Elena Wilson. Quotations from this work are reprinted by permission of Farrar, Straus and Giroux.

Hereafter, references to these works will be given by title only.

The quotations on the back of the dust jacket are from the following sources:

Aimee Semple McPherson: From an account of her self-defense during the famous "kidnapping" episode in 1926, as given by Lately Thomas, *The Vanishing Evangelist.* New York: The Viking Press, 1959. Copyright © 1959 by Lately Thomas.

Amelia Earhart: Amelia's comment on unnecessary baggage on long distance flights, from her book *The Fun of It,* Chicago: Academy Press Limited, 1977; reprint of the original edition published in 1932.

Martha Graham: Graham's reply to a young fan's inquiry about the "meaning" of a new dance, from *The Notebooks of Martha Graham.* New York: Harcourt, Brace, Jovanovich, 1973. Copyright © 1973 by Martha Graham.

Edna St. Vincent Millay: From a letter to poet Arthur Davison Ficke, as found in *Letters of Edna St. Vincent Millay.* Edited by Allen Ross Macdougall. New York: Harper, 1952. Copyright © by Allen Ross Macdougall.

Dorothy Parker: One of Parker's Round Table quips, quoted in the biography of Parker by John Keats, *You Might As Well Live: The Life and Times of Dorothy Parker.* New York: Simon and Schuster, 1970. Copyright © 1970 by John Keats.

Anita Loos: From a response Loos made to a poem written and dedicated to her by William Empson in 1927. Empson's poem had concluded with the line "a girl can't

go on laughing all the time." To this, Loos's rejoinder was "in those days a girl could actually wake up laughing." The whole matter is discussed in an essay entitled "A Girl Can't Go On Laughing All the Time," *American Heritage,* Extra, 1968.

WHEN LIGHTS BEGAN TO SHOW

The poem printed on the page facing the opening paragraphs of this chapter is Edna St. Vincent Millay's "To the Not Impossible Him." This short poem was a part of Millay's collection *A Few Figs From Thistles,* published in 1920. The independent and bouyant spirit of *A Few Figs* captured the attitude of American women as they entered the challenging decade of the twenties. The text of "To the Not Impossible Him" is quoted from Edna St. Vincent Millay, *Collected Poems,* edited by Norma Millay. New York: Harper and Row, 1956. Reprinted by permission of Harper and Row, Publishers, Inc. Copyright © 1956 by Norma Millay Ellis.

The title of this chapter was suggested by a poem entitled "Afternoon on a Hill," by Edna St. Vincent Millay. The final stanza of that poem reads: "And when lights begin to show / Up from the town, / I will mark which must be mine, / And then start down!" The full text of this poem will be found in Millay's *Collected Poems,* in the edition cited above.

The quotation from Alexis de Tocqueville is taken from his *Democracy in America,* translated by Phillips Bradley, American Past Series, two volumes. New York: Random House, 1944. Reprinted by permission of Random House, Inc.

A vivid description of American women as "custodians of higher culture" in the late nineteenth and early twentieth centuries may be found in Helen Hooven Santmyer, *Ohio Town.* New York: Harper and Row, 1984.

The sense of disillusionment suffered by many American men after the First World War is remembered in Edmund Wilson's *The Twenties.* Wilson's memoir is valuable also for its firsthand comments about the arts, politics, literature, gossip and fashion of the 1920s. Also of interest in this connection is *The Undertaker's Garland,* by Edmund Wilson and John Peale Bishop. New York: Alfred A. Knopf, 1922.

MOVING STARWARD

"Moving starward" is a phrase found in a poem Alfred Stieglitz wrote in 1918, shortly after meeting Georgia O'Keeffe. The poem began: "The flesh is starving / Its soul is moving starward / Seeking its own particular star / A man intercepts . . ." This portion of Stieglitz's poem is quoted in Laurie Lisle's *Portrait of an Artist: A Biography of Georgia O'Keeffe.* New York: Seaview Books, 1980. Reprinted by permission of Seaview Books. Copyright © 1980 by Laurie Lisle.

The quotation from Dorothy Parker's scathing review of Elinor Glyn's *It* is taken from *The Portable Dorothy Parker.*

AIMEE SEMPLE MCPHERSON

The photograph of Aimee Semple McPherson as she appeared on the occasion of her memorable "Rose of Sharon" sermon is from The Associated Press.

Details about the dramatic services conducted by McPherson at Angelus Temple, her words of self-defense before the grand jury in Los Angeles, and the text of the resolution related to her "kidnapping" case by the Church Federation of Los Angeles are cited from Robert Bahr's *Least of All the Saints.* Englewood Cliffs, New Jersey: Prentice-Hall, 1979. Reprinted by permission of Prentice-Hall, Inc. Copyright © 1979 by Robert Bahr.

The portion of Dorothy Parker's review of Aimee Semple McPherson's autobiography *In the Service of the King* is quoted from *The Portable Dorothy Parker.*

Anthony Quinn's autobiographical reminiscences of services he attended as a teenager at Angelus Temple are quoted from his book *The Original Sin: A Self-Portrait.* Boston: Little, Brown and Company, 1972. Reprinted by permission of Little, Brown and Company. Copyright © 1972 by Anthony Quinn.

Further insight into the relation between McPherson and her mother may be found in Lately Thomas, *Storming Heaven: The Lives and Turmoils of Minnie Kennedy and Aimee Semple McPherson.* New York: William Morrow and Company, 1970.

AMELIA EARHART

The photograph of Amelia Earhart as the young "Lady Lindy" is from the archives of The Smithsonian Institution.

Earhart's views about flying as "fun," her advice to young women, and her comments about the restrictions imposed on women by tradition are taken from her book *The Fun of It.* Chicago: Academy Press Limited, 1977; reprint of the original edition published in 1932. Reprinted by permission of Academy Press Limited.

Walter Lippmann's eulogy on Amelia Earhart first appeared in *The New York Herald Tribune.*

All quotations from letters written by Earhart to her friends, her family and her husband, George P. Putnam, are cited from *Letters from Amelia: An Intimate Portrait of Amelia Earhart,* by Jean Backus. Boston: Beacon Press, 1982. Reprinted by permission of Beacon Press. Copyright © 1982 by Jean Backus.

Literary records related to Earhart's final attempt to fly around the world were gathered and arranged, after her disappearance, by George P. Putnam in a book entitled *Last Flight.* New York: Harcourt, Brace and Company, 1937.

For further discussion of Earhart's character and career, see Dick Strippel, *Amelia Earhart: The Myth and the Reality.* Hicksville, New York: Exposition Press, 1972.

MARTHA GRAHAM

The photograph of Martha Graham around the time she gave her first recital of modern dance in 1926 is from The University of Illinois Library.

John Gwen's description of Martha Graham at the Mark Hellinger Theater in New York is taken from his column "Observing Dance," *Dance Magazine,* Volume 48, June, 1974. Reprinted by permission of Danad Publishing Company. Copyright © 1974 by Danad Publishing Company, Inc. Martha Graham's own words about "inhabiting our bodies" are quoted from this same source.

The ancient Christian text from *The Acts of John*—"To the universe belongs the dancer"—is quoted from Elaine Pagels, "To the Universe Belongs the Dancer," *Parabola,* Volume IV:2, May, 1979. Reprinted by permission of the Society for the Study of Myth and Tradition. Copyright © 1979 by the Society for the Study of Myth and Tradition.

Ruth St. Denis's words about her destiny as a dancer are quoted from Suzanne Shelton's *Divine Dancer: A Biography of Ruth St. Denis.* New York: Doubleday and Company, 1981. Reprinted by permission of Doubleday and Company. Copyright © 1981 by Suzanne Shelton. Other allusions to St. Denis, Ted Shawn and the Denishawn School are derived from this same source, as are the program notes for the dance *Egypta.*

Quotations from Martha Graham's 1982 interview in Dallas first appeared in *The Dallas Morning News* and are reprinted here with the kind permission of the interviewer, Mr. Harry Bowman.

The earlier, formative stages of Graham's life and career are discussed in Merle Armitage, editor, *Martha Graham: The Early Years.* Da Capo Series in Dance. New York: Da Capo Press, Inc., 1978.

EDNA ST. VINCENT MILLAY

The photograph of Edna St. Vincent Millay is from the Vassar College Library's collection.

Quotations from Millay's published letters to family, friends and colleagues, are cited from *Letters of Edna St. Vincent Millay.* Edited by Allen Ross Macdougall. New York: Harper, 1952. Reprinted by permission of Harper and Row, Publishers, Inc. Copyright © by Allen Ross Macdougall.

Edmund Wilson's words about Edna St. Vincent Millay as she appeared in the summer of 1948 are quoted from his memoir *The Forties.* New York: Farrar, Straus and Giroux, 1983. Reprinted by permission of Farrar, Straus and Giroux. Copyright © 1983 by Helen Miranda Wilson.

An intriguing account of Millay's early days in New York, when she was associated with the Provincetown Players and with the crowd at *Vanity Fair,* may be found in Anne Cheney, *Millay in Greenwich Village.* Tuscaloosa, Alabama: University of Alabama Press, 1975.

Millay's poem "My Candle Burns at Both Ends," called "First Fig" in many printed versions of her poetry, is quoted from *Collected Poems,* edited by Norma Millay. New York: Harper and Row, 1956. Reprinted by permission of Harper and Row, Publishers, Inc. Copyright ©

1956 by Norma Millay Ellis. All subsequent quotations from Millay's published poetry cited in this chapter are taken from this same source.

The poem fragment written in Edna Millay's notebook, and discovered shortly after her death, is quoted from Vincent Sheean's *The Indigo Bunting: A Memoir of Edna St. Vincent Millay.* New York: Schocken Books, 1973. Published by arrangement with Harper and Row, Publishers. Reprinted by permission of Schocken Books. Copyright © 1951 by Vincent Sheean. Sheean's personal recollections of Millay, alluded to several times in this chapter, are also quoted from this memoir.

Edmund Wilson's description of Millay's extraordinary magnetism and beauty as a young woman is cited from his memoir *The Twenties.* The account of Millay's emotional state at the time of the production of *The King's Henchman* at the Metropolitan Opera in February of 1927 is cited from the same source.

The description of the Millay family—Edna, her mother Cora and her two sisters Norma and Kathleen—on Cape Cod for a summer holiday in 1920 is quoted from Edmund Wilson's *The Shores of Light: A Literary Chronicle of the 1920s and 1930s.* New York: Farrar, Straus and Giroux, 1952. Reprinted by permission of Farrar, Straus and Giroux. Copyright © 1952 by Edmund Wilson.

Millay's activities in Paris during July of 1921 are recounted in a letter of Edmund Wilson to his friend John Peale Bishop. This letter is collected, along with many others from the 1920s, in Wilson's *Letters on Literature and Politics. 1912–1972.* Edited by Elena Wilson. New York: Farrar, Straus and Giroux. Reprinted by permission of Farrar, Straus and Giroux. Copyright © 1975 by Elena Wilson.

The lines from Sappho are quoted from John Frederick Nims, editor, *Sappho to Valéry: Poems in Translation.* New Brunswick, New Jersey: Rutgers University Press, 1971. Reprinted by permission of Rutgers University Press. Copyright © 1971 by Rutgers University, the State University of New Jersey.

Millay's distinctive contributions to American poetry are assessed in Norman A. Brittin's *Edna St. Vincent Millay.* United States Authors Series. Boston: Twayne Publishers, 1967.

DOROTHY PARKER

The photograph of Dorothy Parker taken during her heyday as the most quotable woman in New York is from Culver Pictures.

Lillian Hellman's recollections of Dorothy Parker are quoted from Hellman's memoir *An Unfinished Woman.* Boston: Little, Brown and Company, 1969. Reprinted by permission of Little, Brown and Company. Copyright © 1969 by Lillian Hellman.

All quotations in this chapter from Parker's poetry, fiction and book reviews are cited from the omnibus collection *The Portable Dorothy Parker.*

Quotations from the famous *Paris Review* interview with Dorothy Parker are cited from *Writers at Work.* First Series. Edited by Malcolm Cowley. New York: The Viking Press, 1958. Reprinted by permission of The Vik-

ing Press. Copyright © 1957, 1958 by The Paris Review, Inc.

The recollections of Frank Crowninshield, Donald Ogden Stewart, Robert Benchley and others associated with Parker at *Vogue, Vanity Fair* and the Algonquin Round Table are cited from John Keats's *You Might As Well Live: The Life and Times of Dorothy Parker.* New York: Simon and Schuster, 1970. Reprinted by permission of Simon and Schuster. Copyright © 1970 by John Keats. Excerpts from reviews of Parker's poetry by Genevieve Taggard and Alexander Woollcott are quoted from the same source.

Anita Loos's lampoon of the Algonquin Round Table's members is taken from her novel *But Gentlemen Marry Brunettes.* New York: Boni and Liveright, 1928. Reprinted by permission.

Diana Forbes-Robertson's comments about Parker's drinking habits—as well as George Oppenheimer's story about luring Parker into a proofreading session with a bottle of whiskey—are cited from John Keats, *You Might As Well Live.*

Edmund Wilson's early recollection of Parker as "overperfumed" is quoted from his memoir *The Twenties.*

Parker's comment that Hollywood "smells like a laundry" originally appeared in the *New York World Telegram and Sun* in 1953.

A short, appreciative analysis of Parker's importance as an American writer may be found in Arthur F. Kinney, *Dorothy Parker.* United States Authors Series. Number 315. Boston: Twayne Publishers, 1978.

ANITA LOOS

The photograph of Anita Loos in the twenties is one which, according to H.L. Mencken, "made me yodel." Photo courtesy of Anita Loos.

During her long and active life, Anita Loos wrote several versions of her experiences in Hollywood, of the people she knew, the places she went, and the situations she found herself involved in. Two of these memoirs are used throughout this chapter as basic sources for Anita Loos's words and recollections: *A Girl Like I,* New York: The Viking Press, 1966; and *Kiss Hollywood Good-by,* New York: The Viking Press, 1974. Quotations are reprinted by permission of The Viking Press. Copyright © 1966, 1974 by Anita Loos.

Loos had not only a career in Hollywood as an actress and screenwriter but a career in fiction as well. Her two most famous works in this genre were: *Gentlemen Prefer Blondes,* New York: Boni and Liveright, 1925; and its sequel, *But Gentlemen Marry Brunettes,* New York: Boni and Liveright, 1928. Quotations from these works are cited with permission.